Sarah Doudney

Under Gray Walls

Sarah Doudney

Under Gray Walls

ISBN/EAN: 9783337016029

Printed in Europe, USA, Canada, Australia, Japan

Cover: Foto ©ninafisch / pixelio.de

More available books at **www.hansebooks.com**

UNDER GRAY WALLS.

BY

SARAH DOUDNEY,

AUTHOR OF "FAITH HARROWBY," "THE BEAUTIFUL ISLAND," ETC.

> "But while I dreamed of God's eternal home
> Watching the shadows as they flitted by,
> Voices all dear and earnest seemed to come
>   From out the grave and sky.
>
> Bidding me work while it is called To-day;
> To suffer if He will, and so be strong;
> To use His blessed gifts as best I may,
>   For no true life is long."
>
> Autumn Memories.

LONDON:
SUNDAY SCHOOL UNION,
56, OLD BAILEY, E.C.

NEW YORK: THOMAS NELSON AND SONS,
42, BLEECKER STREET.

1871.

CONTENTS.

CHAP.		PAGE
I.	Poor Jack	1
II.	The Ruby Ring	9
III.	Mrs. Cravenhurst	16
IV.	School	25
V.	St. Agatha's College	33
VI.	Change	43
VII.	Christmas	50
VIII.	My New Life begins	57
IX.	My New Life	63
X.	Living for Self	69
XI.	Dark Clouds	75
XII.	"Right dear in the sight of the Lord is the death of His saints"	84
XIII.	A Strange Meeting	90
XIV.	A Confession and an Illness	98
XV.	Conclusion	105

UNDER GRAY WALLS.

CHAPTER I.

Poor Jack.

What a keen wind! I can hear it whistle sharply through the boughs of the old elms; and looking up I descry the great untidy nests of the rooks among those naked branches. The rooks! how they wheel and circle and caw; now coming near, and now drifting so far away that their black bodies look like splashes of ink upon the clear blue sky! To me there is something homely in their strange, harsh clamour. And if I were ever to be miles and miles away from Priorsbury, the caw of a rook would call back my thoughts to these old elm-tops, and the tall cathedral spire.

Thus I muse (only in a more disjointed fashion), basking in a broad patch of sunshine close to the cathedral wall. The fresh morning light shows all the dinginess of my coarse brown linsey frock, and all the rustiness of my little black cloth cloak; but what does that matter to me? Perhaps by-and-by I shall have a new summer dress, when the trees have got theirs. At present I think they are looking quite as shabby as I do.

It is a morning in early March; the daffodils are as yet only in bud, but there are clusters of snowdrops among the green mounds; and I, little Bessie Mere, leaning against a gray headstone, muse about the pale drooping flowers which seem to be always discoursing of sorrowful things to each other. Growing tired of them, I steal a glance at the tall gentleman, brown and handsome, who is loitering just within the shadow of the western door. Then, hearing a sound of rustling skirts, I turn my head sharply to look at the lady who is coming towards him.

She has the saddest, palest face I have ever seen. Her beauty and her sorrow touch me in some mysterious fashion, and bring tears into my eyes. I watch the pair with something more than mere childish curiosity, and am near enough to catch a few words of their talk.

"You know we are to sail on the tenth, Clara?" says the gentleman, very quietly.

"Yes," she answers. "Do you think it will be long before the war is over?"

"I fear it will; I don't fancy the Russians will give in without a hard fight."

Her head droops lower, and my little heart begins to throb. They are speaking of that great struggle which has only just commenced, and of which I have heard my father talking to Aunt Esther. And I understand, all at once, something of the mighty cost of war. My tears come thick and fast, I can scarcely keep down my sobs, but I resolve to slip away from the spot unobserved, for I have an instinctive consciousness that these two imagine themselves to be alone. So I run off unnoticed, my small feet treading noiselessly over the soft turf.

I hasten homewards, still sobbing, for this is my first glimpse of a real sorrow, and I take it to heart as if it were my own. One or two persons look compassionately at my tearful face, but I hurry on unheeding, and turn down into our narrow street. Here there is a perpetual dusk, for the tall gloomy houses shut out the sunlight, and the mouldering old walls wear the saddest gray tints. I enter our shop-door, flanked with piles of dingy drab and brown books, and overturning a basketful of dusty pamphlets, rush on into the little sitting-room. But then I stop short, for a great surprise awaits me.

My father is in his accustomed chair by the fire, and a man in a red coat sits by his side. I cannot see the stranger's face distinctly, for his back is turned towards the light, but his hand rests upon my father's shoulder, and he speaks in a low voice. At the sight of me, Aunt Esther calls out tremulously, "Here's little Bessie! Come and speak to your brother Jack, my dear."

"I didn't know I had a brother," I respond, in utter bewilderment.

"Bessie," says the red-coated man, holding out his

arms, "you'll give the poor soldier a kiss, won't you? I'm going off to the war, darling—and perhaps—perhaps I may never come back."

I am too much astonished to reply, but I let him hold me close to his breast, and kiss me again and again.

"She is very like mother," he exclaims, after a pause. "Poor dear mother! O dad, if she could only come back for an hour, to hear me say I'm sorry for all the harm I've done! Yet it's better as it is; there are thousands of mothers crying over their lads to-day. Nothing but partings, dad, nothing but partings!"

My father gives a suppressed sob, and the soldier talks on excitedly.

"Don't fret, dear old daddy; it's harder for some folks than for us. There's my captain,—Captain Ashburn, you know—in sad trouble. I'm his servant, and he's the best fellow in the world. Well, he is engaged to a beautiful young lady who lives in this city. Her name is Miss Severn, and he's here to-day to take leave of her."

Was it Captain Ashburn and Miss Severn who had met under the cathedral walls? Ah, what a dreadful thing this war must be; it is breaking so many hearts! I burst out into sudden tears, hiding my face on my brother's scarlet breast; and then we all weep together.

Jack went back to his quarters on the evening of the same day. His regiment was stationed at Portsmouth, and on the tenth of March he was to sail. For the first and last time in my life, I saw my soldier brother in that little sitting-room behind the shop, and of his previous history I knew nothing. That he had committed great faults, I cannot doubt; but I would fain hope that death was to him the dawning of a better existence, and that the penitent soul found rest and forgiveness at last. My father and mother had been married very early in life: Jack was their eldest child, and I was the youngest. A number of other little ones had filled up the gap between us two, but they all had died in infancy; and the first-born was destined to bring nothing but sorrow to his parents, from the cradle to the grave. And yet, as my father was wont to say afterwards, he made a noble end.

Frequent letters came to us from the seat of war, and we looked out eagerly for the daily papers. In my eyes, this soldier brother of mine had already become a hero as grand as any of the dead-and-gone warriors of olden times; and I longed for the far-off day when he should return to us covered with honours. In these dreams Aunt Esther encouraged me, for her sanguine temperament led her always to take a bright view of things, and Jack was an old favourite of hers, despite his errors. She was fond of depicting the glorious future which she believed to be in store for him, and gave free expression to her anticipations.

"The black sheep of the family often becomes a credit to the flock," she would remark, with an air of conviction. "We shall see the lad wear his epaulets before we are in our graves, Thomas!"

But my father's sole answer was ever a gentle shake of the head, accompanied by a sad smile.

The summer was fast gliding away, and in September, just when the Virginian creeper had put on its warmest, mellowest crimson, and the yew berries had ripened in the Close,—the battle of the Alma was fought and won. I can remember to this day the rapture and the triumph those tidings brought to our quiet city, and how groups of people stood at street corners to discuss the news. Then Jack's letter reached us, giving a detailed account of this his first action, and making special mention of "his dear master," Captain Ashburn, who had borne himself gallantly during that three hours and a half of desperate fighting. Both had come out of the encounter unscathed, and there was heart-felt rejoicing in our small home-circle.

October came, and golden leaves dropped softly upon the graves under the gray cathedral walls. Filmy webs of gossamer drifted about in the still air, and I wondered if the fairies,—in whom I half believed,—had grown tired of their summer mantles and cast them away. Wheat was sown in the rich brown furrows, and the faithless swallows took their departure. Only two more months, and then that memorable year would be at an end.

Another victory was gained. The name of Balaklava was passed from lip to lip, and the charge of the Six Hundred became an oft-told tale. There was a letter from Jack, briefer than the last, but telling us all we wanted to know. He and his captain were safe and well.

November set in, and moaning winds began to strip

the cathedral elms; the chilly twilight shortened the days, and clouds of gray mist gathered over the familiar landscape around Priorsbury. I went back to my old winter corner by the fireside, and hungered for more news from the Crimea.

The story of that terrible struggle at Inkermann came to us at last; and then, on a certain bleak morning, I came down to breakfast, and found my father sitting silently with an open letter in his hand. Aunt Esther stood beside him, leaning her head against the chimney-piece and sobbing audibly; and I, pausing in the doorway, felt a consciousness of the sad truth strike suddenly upon my heart.

"It's all over with him, Bessie," said my father, turning towards me with a face of patient sorrow. "But he did his duty like a brave man. God bless him!"

He broke down all at once, and when I ran to him and put my arms round his neck, the tears were streaming over his furrowed cheeks. It was long before my mute caresses soothed and comforted him, although he held me in his arms with a strong close clasp, as if he feared to lose me too. And then Aunt Esther, picking up the letter which had dropped upon the floor, read me the brief account of my brother's death, written by one of his comrades.

Jack had been cut down in defending the prostrate body of his captain, and had given his own life for the master he loved so well. But the sacrifice was in vain, for Captain Ashburn was mortally wounded, and lived only a few hours after his removal from the spot where he fell.

The weeks passed on, and we three went about our daily business as if nothing had happened, but my father grew grayer and older, and leaned heavily on his stick when he walked, and I knew that the blow had fallen upon him with a crushing force. We had not many intimate acquaintances among our neighbours, and very few people knew of the loss we had sustained. And in the meanwhile, hundreds of other homes were made desolate, and the long, long siege of Sebastopol dragged on as if it would never come to an end.

But there came a day when the cathedral bells clashed out joyously, peal after peal, and at night there were illuminations and bonfires, for the great fortress was won at last. We sat in our quiet room, hearing the sounds of rejoicing and festivity, and thinking of that voice of wailing which must always blend with the shouts of victory. But we said little to each other, and if Aunt Esther's tears flowed fast, they were silently wiped away.

CHAPTER II.

THE RUBY RING.

PEACE had been proclaimed; the allied forces were withdrawn from the Russian territories. The excitement was ended, and public feeling began to subside into a more settled state; while our old city of Priorsbury was fast sinking back into its usual condition of drowsy dignity. But from this respectable torpor it was destined to be roused into busy gossip by the marriage of its new Dean, Dr. Cravenhurst.

Every one was taken by surprise, for the Dean was long past fifty, and the lady of his choice had only seen four-and-twenty summers. Many of the good citizens were somewhat scandalized at this disparity of age, and went so far as to aver that the match was a most unsuitable one. Others, however, maintained that the Dean had an undoubted right to please himself; and that no one could blame a penniless orphan like Clara Severn for leaving an uncomfortable home to be a good man's wife. For the bride was dependent on the charity of her uncle, the Reverend Charles Severn, who had daughters of his own. Priorsbury talked itself hoarse about the matter, and even Aunt Esther said, with a sigh—

"Well, well; one couldn't expect the poor young thing to mourn for Captain Ashburn all her days. And I'm told that her cousins have always pecked at her ever since she has lived under their father's roof."

The marriage was a very quiet one; there were no bridesmaids, no wedding-chimes. The bride stood at the altar in her plain travelling-dress. And when the honeymoon was over, and the pair returned to the Deanery, Mrs. Cravenhurst settled down into her new position as easily and naturally as if she had no idea of the sensation she had created in the city. Her visitors found her perfectly self-possessed, and quite at home in the old-fashioned house under the cathedral walls.

From the day when I had seen her taking that last farewell of her lover, Clara Severn had become a heroine of mine. I had delighted in picturing her future life, framing a kind of Eden, wherein she and Captain Ashburn were to dwell together, on his return from the war. It was a sore disappointment when my little romance came utterly to an end; and my heroine, quietly accepting the substantial comforts offered her, seemed as calmly contented with her lot as if Captain Ashburn had never lived, and died.

One April morning I sat musing over the few events in my short life, and thinking especially about Mrs. Cravenhurst. As usual, I had resorted to my favourite haunt among the mounds under the cathedral walls, and was contemplating the golden glory of the daffodils to my heart's content. There were violets, too, purple and white, peeping shyly out of their mossy beds at the tree-roots, and scenting the light restless winds that swept over them. Perched on the corner of an old square tomb, so gray and lichen-grown that its inscription could not be traced, I revelled in the general freshness and greenness around me. Presently a lark, singing far aloft, tempted me to gaze straight up at the little black speck hovering near the golden edges of a snowy cloud, until my eyes, dazzled by the brightness, were glad to rest upon the grass at my feet. And there, twinkling among the green blades, was something that looked like a fiery dewdrop.

For a second or two I believed that my sight had played me a trick; but the red spark still glittered on the sod, and I stooped to examine it more closely. It proved to be a brilliant stone set in a ring, and little as I knew of the value of such things, I felt I had found a prize. My heart throbbed fast, my face flushed, and I slipped the ring on my finger with a childish delight in seeing myself so richly adorned. And then my excitement suddenly cooled down when I remembered that my first duty was to seek for the owner. Full of this idea, I rose from my seat, holding the jewel safely hidden in my closed hand, and ran home at full speed. As on a former occasion, I whisked in through the shop-door, coming suddenly into contact with a man who carried a roll of printed bills.

"Hallo!" cried he, good-humouredly. "I hope I haven't knocked the breath out of this little body!"

I frowned at him in reply, and my father shook his

head, saying, "Ah, Bessie, when *will* you learn to walk steadily?"

"I've picked up something very valuable," said I, with offended dignity. "And I want to find out who it belongs to."

"Hallo!" cried the man again. "It isn't Mrs. Cravenhurst's ruby ring, is it?"

"It *is* a ring," I answered; "but I don't know the name of the stone in it."

"Let me look at it, missy," exclaimed the man, putting down his bills.

"No," returned I, stoutly. "I'm going to show it to my father."

My father left his place behind the counter, and came to me at once; Aunt Esther quitted the sitting-room and joined the group.

"That's the ring identical, and no mistake!" said the strange man, who was resolved to have a look at it. "I needn't take the trouble to go on handing about these bills, Mr. Mere. Your little maid has found it, sure enough; and a lucky thing for her." With that he took himself out of the shop, and we three adjourned to our small parlour.

"It belongs to the Dean's lady, Bessie," said my father, when he had heard all the particulars of my finding the treasure. "You must take it to her when you have had your dinner. She has offered a reward of twenty shillings, but I'd rather you didn't accept the money."

"Twenty shillings would be very useful to the child, brother," put in Aunt Esther.

"I know that; but I don't want my little girl to be paid for doing a simple act of duty. There's something degrading in the idea."

"I should feel as you do in the matter, if money were more plentiful with us," rejoined my aunt. "But that frock of Bessie's is terribly shabby, and I should like to get her a new one."

"Let Bessie settle the question," said my father, suddenly turning to me. "Do you want to take Mrs. Cravenhurst's reward or not? Think it over, dearie, before you answer."

I stood still and considered. Visions of a new frock danced before my eyes, and I was tempted to utter an affirmative. But I loved my father better than all the frocks in the world, and I had a consciousness that such a reply would mortify him. In addition to this, I too was not destitute of a certain kind of dignity, which must be outraged if I were paid for being honest.

"No," I said aloud. "I won't have the reward." And my father drew me towards him for a kiss.

Aunt Esther said nothing to shake my resolution, but clearing away her needlework, prepared to set out the dinner. We kept no servant, and our meal was as simple as can well be imagined; but cleanliness and good cooking can do wonders, and our plain fare was always wholesome and palatable. Yet hungry as I really was, the thought of going to the Deanery almost took away my appetite.

"Suppose I should see the Dean himself, daddy," I said.

"Well, Bessie; you have never done him any harm, have you?"

"Oh, no; of course not."

"Then why should you object to see him? We ought not to fear meeting those whom we have never injured."

"I don't think I quite fear him; but he's such a great man, isn't he, father?"

"He is a learned man, certainly; and he holds a high position in life. Yet, Bessie, if you are a member of Christ's kingdom, you are equal with him in the sight of God. But go and make yourself tidy, my dear, and set off with the ring. I shan't feel easy till the lady has got back her property."

I ran up to my little garret, and was speedily followed by Aunt Esther, who brushed my hair with her own hands.

"You look very nice, Bessie," said she, in a tone of motherly approval, as she smoothed my shabby bonnet-strings. "I don't need to caution you as to your behaviour, for you were always a well-mannered child. Just be your own natural little self, that's all."

I carefully slipped the ring inside the palm of my glove, and went my way. My father and Aunt Esther stood at the shop-door, and watched me as far as the corner of the street.

I tripped on lightly and cheerily until I came to the massive iron gates of the Close; and there I paused to consider in what terms I should decline the promised reward. I must not refuse bluntly, but modestly and steadily; and as no set form of words occurred to me at that moment, I passed on through the gates, a little doubtful what to say.

Then I entered the cloisters, turning out of them into a long, narrow alley paved with footworn stones. On my left was the range of ancient houses occupied by the clergy connected with the cathedral; and on my right, the high stone wall shutting in the gardens of the bishop's palace. Arriving at the end of this passage, I came to an iron gate which stood open; and going in, I found myself on the smoothly-shaven lawn in front of the Deanery.

CHAPTER III.

Mrs. Cravenhurst.

It was a beautiful old house, the walls, where they were not draperied with ivy, being of the softest, mellowest gray; it had quaint mullioned windows, and a doorway that was like the porch of a church. Tall elms and beeches rose behind it, shadowing its pointed gables and fantastic chimneys; and the rooks clamoured over it noisily, as if they had a right to the place, and were challenging all new comers to dispute their claims. Their familiar voices seemed to make the quiet dignity of the mansion less oppressive, and helped me to conquer a sudden attack of bashfulness. I walked straight up to the massive door, which was thickly studded with great iron nails, and peered about for a bell-handle. At last I found one, half hidden by clustering ivy leaves, and ventured to give it a timid pull.

It produced such a startling peal, that I drew back in affright. A loud, sonorous ring that seemed to echo through the house, and which must, I thought, give the Dean's household the impression that a person of much consequence was impatient to be admitted. The colour rushed into my cheeks at the sound of approaching steps; and then the door was opened by a portly man-servant, who stood silently looking down at me for a second or two.

"Can I see Mrs. Cravenhurst, please?" said I, plucking up heart. "I've found her ring."

"O yes," he answered, smiling benevolently.

I followed him through the dim hall, and past the foot of the wide staircase, to a door at which he paused to knock. A voice from within answered softly, and he entered to tell my errand.

In another moment he had retired, leaving me face to face with a lady who sat near the window. She was seated in a quaint, high-backed chair, and had a small work-table in front of her. My first glance took in little beyond the soft folds of the dove-coloured skirts trailing over the floor; but when she spoke I lifted my eyes and looked at her.

"So you have brought my ring," she said pleasantly.

Some voices seem to have a quieting influence, and Mrs. Cravenhurst's was one of these. The gentle tones set me quite at ease in a moment, and I took the ring out of my glove, telling her where and how it was found.

She received it with evident pleasure, turning it round and round, and slipping it on her finger. And now I had leisure to study the beautiful features I had sometimes admired afar off. I was a child then and have looked on many fair faces since that

C

day, but never on one so lovely as that of Clara Cravenhurst.

She had large brown eyes, soft, yet clear, and her eyebrows and lashes were very dark. Her skin was smooth and white, rarely tinted with any flush; her features were clearly cut, the sweet mouth drooped slightly at the corners, and the shape of the face was perfectly oval. The hair grew very low upon the forehead, in full rich waves of brown, and was gathered up into a sort of knot at the back of the head. I have tried to give some idea of the outer aspect of my life-long friend, because her picture is photographed on my memory, and I love to dwell upon it.

"I had been roaming about under the cathedral walls, hunting for violets, last Wednesday," said Mrs. Cravenhurst after a pause. "It was not until I returned to the house that I missed my ring; it was too large and must have slipped off. And now," she added with a kindly smile, "I will gladly give you the promised reward as well as many thanks."

The dreaded moment had come at last, but much to my own surprise I was equal to the occasion. I spoke clearly and without embarrassment.

"You're very kind ma'am; but if you please, I'd rather not take the money. My father doesn't like me to be paid for doing my duty; and indeed I shouldn't feel comfortable to have that twenty shillings."

Having said these words I was about to take my leave, when Mrs. Cravenhurst detained me.

"But you have done me a very great service my child, and I am really indebted to you. This ring was a gift from the Dean, and its loss vexed me exceedingly. Won't you give me the pleasure of doing something for you in return?"

"No ma'am thank you, I don't want anything; and I'm very glad to have brought the ring back to you."

The lady's eyes travelled all over my dress, from my faded straw bonnet down to my well-worn boots. I did not shrink from her scrutiny; my clothes, although shabby, were clean and neat. Yet something in my aspect must have touched her, it may have been that my little jacket seemed too thin to protect me against the sharp April winds, for her voice was tremulous when she spoke again.

"What is your name, my dear?"

"Bessie Mere, ma'am."

"Mere," she repeated, "Bessie Mere! Had you a relation who was killed in the late war?"

The sweet dark eyes grew strangely eager as she awaited my reply.

"Yes ma'am; my poor brother Jack. He tried to save his master, Captain Ashburn, and——"

"I know, I know," she interrupted. "He was my cousin, Captain Ashburn. Tell me all about yourself my child. O you don't know how glad I am to have met you!"

"We live in Prior's Row," I said. "Father, Aunt Esther and I. Mother is dead, and there were only Jack and me living out of all her children. Jack came to say good-bye before he went away to the war, and we all cried together. He told us what a good master his captain was, the best fellow in the world, he called him."

"Go on," she whispered, "go on!"

"Jack wasn't hurt in the battle of the Alma, nor yet at the other place——"

"Balaklava."

"Yes, that's it. O ma'am, haven't you heard the story? Father has got the letter from one of Jack's comrades, telling all about it."

Mrs. Cravenhurst was sobbing. I felt her tears on my face as she kissed me, and I began to weep too.

"I must go and see your father; I must read that letter. O my child, I must be your friend!" She could say no more; her whole frame shook and quivered as she tried to quiet herself. Suddenly, on the other side of the room a door opened, and in came the Dean.

"Clara, what is the matter? What has happened?" he asked, coming to her side.

She sprang up from her seat, and taking his hand led him back into the room he had just quitted. The door closed upon them, and for some moments I stood listening to the murmur of their voices, and wondering whether I was to remain or depart?

Presently the Dean came back alone. He was a stout dignified-looking man, with a fine face and keen gray eyes; but those same eyes softened when he addressed me, and I quite forgot to be awed by him.

"God gives us all sorrows and afflictions in common."

"Go home now, my little girl," he said, laying his hand kindly on my shoulder. "Mrs. Cravenhurst is not well, but she will see you again by-and-by. We shan't forget you, rest assured of that."

Through the dim hall and out of the heavy oaken door I went with my brain in a whirl. Over the smooth green lawn, on into the paved alley, while the bells chimed musically for afternoon service; and into the cloisters, among the square caps and white surplices of the prebendaries. Then passing the iron gates, I mingled once more with the tide of human life flowing along the high street of the populous old city. There was a customer in our shop when I returned, an old man overhauling piles of worm-eaten volumes, and my father was not at liberty to listen to my story.

But I poured it all into Aunt Esther's ears, and related it again before tea. My hearers were deeply moved, and the tears stood in their eyes when I described the scene that had taken place. Yet my father smiled a little when I told him I had not found the Dean at all terrible.

"Ah Bessie," said he, as though reading what he was about to say from a book which he held in his hand, "God gives us all sorrows and afflictions in common, that the members of His great human family may be drawn closely together. He is no respecter of persons."

On the very next day Mrs. Cravenhurst fulfilled her promise of coming to see us. But she did not again lose her composure, although her self-command was sorely tried. She sat in our little parlour reading the letter from poor Jack's comrade in utter silence; and then refolding it, and putting in back into its envelope, she talked calmly to my father about his son's death. She had heard the story of my brother's bravery and devotion from other sources, she told us; but the simple language used by this soldier friend of his made it wonderfully real to her.

"We shall meet again, Bessie," she said when she took her departure. "From henceforth you are my little friend, you know; and I shall have a right to interest myself about you, shall I not?"

CHAPTER IV.

School.

Y new friend paid us another visit shortly after the first, and the object of this call took us all by surprise. She asked my father's permission to put me to a good school, and have me educated for a governess.

She came out with this proposal simply and frankly, just as I have stated it here; telling us that she had talked the matter over with the Dean, and had come to the conclusion that she could not serve me so well in any other way. And she alluded in a few words to the strange sad bond which united her to our family, making us understand that she felt a deep sense of satisfaction in being of use to us.

It was therefore arranged that I should go daily for general instruction to a widow lady in Priorsbury, who was desirous of receiving a limited number of pupils; and when I had attained the age of fifteen, I was to be sent to finish my education at a first-rate school in the neighbourhood. My studies were to begin after Easter, and I looked forward to them with infinite delight, for

I had always been fond of learning, and many of my happiest hours were spent in poring over the old books in the shop. My father, who although self-educated, was a man of no ordinary ability, was wont to encourage my love of literature, and had already instructed me in geography and history. On some subjects I was unusually well-informed for a girl of my years, while on others I was profoundly ignorant. Of accomplishments I knew nothing whatever, and with the works of great modern authors I was but little acquainted. And when I thought of all that was in store for me, I felt like a traveller about to explore unknown regions, rich with untold treasures.

One bright May morning I tripped along the stone-paved alley in the Close, to pay a visit to the Deanery. Above me was the sweet green shadow of the leaf-laden boughs; over the old wall trailed the golden tresses of the laburnum; and the scented lilacs tossed their plumes among the delicate red and white apple-blossoms. The prebendaries' windows were opened to admit the balmy air, and within, the rooms were gay with flowers in pots and stands. There was a loud singing of canaries behind their prison bars of gilded wire, and the finches and thrushes responded from their perches on the trees. The whole alley was filled with perfume and music; and as for me, my old shyness appeared to have taken flight with the bleak weather. My shabby frock was replaced by a neat and pretty dress, the gift of Mrs. Cravenhurst; I had a new bonnet and new boots, and it seemed as if my life had put on a new aspect altogether.

This time I did not quake at the clamorous peal of the Dean's door-bell. The portly man-servant conducted me at once to his mistress's presence, and she stretched forth her hand with words of kindly welcome.

"Sit down opposite to me, Bessie," she said. "I want to look at you and talk to you at the same time."

I obeyed, placing myself on the other side of the little work-table, and letting my glance dwell lovingly on the sweet face of my benefactress.

"You know, my child," she continued, dropping her embroidery on her lap, "that you are not to be Mrs. Redmond's only pupil. There are five little girls besides yourself."

"Yes, ma'am."

"And do you like the idea of having companions?"

"I think I do," I answered musingly, "but I have been very much alone."

"It is not well for a child to associate only with grown people," rejoined Mrs. Cravenhurst; "yet you must be prepared to put up with some small annoyances, Bessie; school-girls are fond of teasing."

"I haven't been used to teasing, ma'am; but I'll try and bear it good-humouredly."

"Then you will be a wise little woman. And you mustn't be wounded, my child, if silly and even spiteful things are said by those who may consider their station in life higher than your own. Never be ashamed because foolish people may call you lowly born. Remember that she who tries earnestly to do her duty as a Christian, and strives to be kind and courteous to all, is the true gentlewoman."

"I should like to be a lady," I said.

"The best bred people are those who are most considerate of the feelings of others," replied Mrs. Cravenhurst earnestly. "The golden rule — you know it Bessie—is a better guide to good manners than all the books on etiquette that ever were published."

I was to begin my schooling on the morrow, and these wise words of counsel, so gently and tenderly spoken, strengthened me greatly. I went homewards with a light heart, and spent the rest of the day in writing copies and working out sums; and more than once I found myself wondering how far the attainments of my new companions would exceed my own.

The next morning found me seated in a pleasant room, overlooking a bright strip of garden ground. Five other girls sat with me at the long deal table, and Mrs. Redmond, a lady of some thirty years, presided over our studies with a quiet firmness and gentle decision which soon taught us to yield to her influence. At my right hand sat Ida Sedgeworth, a fragile fair-faced girl of my own age, whose evident nervousness made her an object of compassion to me. She appeared to be considerably behind the rest of us in general information, and more than once her mistakes excited a suppressed titter, which Mrs. Redmond instantly checked. I saw her blue eyes flash, and her delicate cheeks flush with pain and anger, when she became conscious of her companions' ill-timed mirth. And I formed then and there the hasty resolution to be her friend and champion.

At one o'clock we had a lunch of bread and butter, and at three the day's studies came to an end. Then Mrs. Redmond took leave of us, with many injunctions to be punctual on the morrow, and we prepared to quit the house. My hat of coarse brown straw and my plain cape were speedily donned, and I thought that one or two of the girls looked a little scornfully at my attire. But Ida Sedgeworth's clothes were as simple as my own, and certainly her frock was far shabbier than the one I was now wearing.

"How tiresome!" she cried fretfully, as she tugged at the strings which fastened her cloak. "Here's a knot, and I can't undo it."

I was about to offer my aid, when another girl with a pleasant face stepped up to her. "Let me try, Ida," said she.

She did try, patiently enough, for a few seconds; but the knot was an obstinate one, and Ida wriggled and twisted under her hands.

"You're a long time about it, Ellen," she said at last. "I think you've made it worse." It was an ungracious speech, and the others instantly resented it.

"Let her help herself, Ellen," cried more than one voice.

"You're all very unkind," retorted Ida, reddening, and pulling herself away from Ellen's fingers.

"Come along, Nelly," said the tallest and oldest of our party, taking the arm of the girl addressed. "Ida

Sedgeworth always was a peevish little thing ever since I've known her." And they all departed, leaving me alone with my troubled schoolfellow. Tears were now falling fast down her thin cheeks, and my sympathies were thoroughly aroused. I went up to her, and proffered my help in such an earnest tone, that she stopped crying in sheer surprise.

"Thank you," she responded briefly; and the knot soon yielded to my efforts. Then her face brightened, and she began to make friends with me at once.

"We'll always walk home together, won't we?" said she, putting her arm within mine. "They are not a nice set of girls—so rude and disagreeable. Ellen Fletcher is the best of them, but Blanch Lincoln governs her completely. Blanch's papa is rich, you know, and she's so proud."

I did *not* know; my companions were all strangers to me, but they seemed to be pretty well acquainted with each other.

"Where do you live?" asked Ida, abruptly.

"In Prior's Row."

"Why that's a very common place, isn't it? There are no gentlefolks there."

"Oh no," I answered, with a sudden burst of frankness. "Only poor people live in our street; we are poor ourselves. My father keeps a little book shop —not a grand one like Mortimer's in the High Street, but a——"

"Then how can he afford to send you to Mrs. Redmond?" interrupted Ida, stopping short and staring into my face.

"He doesn't pay for me. Mrs. Cravenhurst, the Dean's lady, does that."

" But what makes her do it, you are no relation of hers, I suppose?"

"Oh no, of course not."

"Well then ; what *does* make her do it?"

Ida was determined to have an answer. I hesitated; somehow I did not feel willing to tell my new acquaintance the story of Mrs. Cravenhurst's loss. I had an idea that endless questions would follow my revelation, and the subject seemed too sacred to be lightly discussed. I wanted to cover it up reverently, and put it out of sight.

"Just because she is good and kind and took a liking to me," I replied.

"But how did she first see you?"

"I picked up her ruby ring, and carried it to the Deanery. She had dropped it under the cathedral walls."

"Ah!" said my companion, musingly, "I wish some rich lady would patronise me. My papa is a gentleman, and as good as anybody in Priorsbury, but he's poor. He has to scrape and save to get me educated, I can tell you; and that's why I'm always so meanly dressed. It's a sad pity."

I agreed that it was a pity. It seemed natural for me to expend my sympathy on Ida,—a delicate little lady in distressed circumstances.

"I'm very sorry for you," I said; "but perhaps you'll grow rich some day. Who knows?"

"I don't think that's likely," she replied. "My

father is on bad terms with his elder brother, who has all the family property. And Uncle Michael took a second wife and had several children, on purpose to spite papa."

By this time we had reached the corner of Prior's Row, where we parted. And in my old impetuous fashion I rushed down the narrow street, impatient to tell Aunt Esther all about my new friend.

CHAPTER V.

St. Agatha's College.

The time passed away very pleasantly during this period of my life. I made rapid progress in my studies, thereby giving great satisfaction to those who were interested in me; and Mrs. Redmond soon discovered that I possessed a decided taste for music. To sing was my greatest delight; and I was allowed to go constantly to the Deanery to practise on Mrs. Cravenhurst's piano. It was a happy time, and the days and months sped swiftly by.

Being much in Mrs. Cravenhurst's company I used to watch her closely, storing up all her delicate little ways for future imitation. I copied, as nearly as possible, her manner and mode of speech; and my intense love and admiration for her helped me much in this. She was my model—the best and sweetest one that an unformed girl ever studied to her own improvement.

There were, however, some few thorns among my roses. Blanch Lincoln was bitterly jealous of me—angry to find herself left behind by one who was two years her junior. Then too, my persistent championship of Ida Sedgeworth sometimes got me into disfavour with the rest, for she was by no means popular in our small community. Her disposition was peevish and fretful; ready to take offence, and to shed floods of tears on the smallest provocation. It may have been her weakness that rendered her dear to my stronger nature, and led me to shield her from all vexation, as far as lay in my power. For I did love her very heartily, encouraging her to lean on me, and depend on my aid, until I became, as the girls were wont to say, "A slave to her whims." Sometimes I went to her home, a little house in a retired neighbourhood, where her father kept up that proud struggle with poverty which a gentleman of small means understands but too well. Mr. Sedgeworth was a tall thin man, with a stoop in his shoulders, which somehow gave me the idea that he was carrying Sindbad's Old Man of the Sea; and the weight of his invisible burden seemed to make him prematurely old and gray. He devoted himself to the fragile little daughter who tyrannised over him.

There was another member of this household who was equally subservient to Ida's caprices, and this was an old Scotch woman. Nurse Murray's affection for her young lady was repaid in a strange, fitful way; sometimes by extravagant fondness, sometimes by ungracious words, and often by utter indifference. But nothing seemed to alter the good creature's love for her charge.

Once or twice Ida accompanied me to the Deanery,

but Mrs. Cravenhurst was not disposed to share my liking for my new friend. She freely admitted that the girl's frail health, and her father's limited means, were no light trials; yet she argued that Ida made the most of her miseries, and overlooked her blessings. "Our happiness in life," she would say, "depended in a great measure upon ourselves."

"I am speaking out of my own experience, Bessie dear," she added. "I have had great sorrows, but consolations always came too. You may be sure that whenever we find a sharp thorn in our path, God has planted a heartsease somewhere very near it."

It was a great truth, and I doubt not that Clara Cravenhurst's inner life furnished her with many such instances of the Divine love.

We never spoke again of those two graves lying far away in the Crimea. As if by mutual consent the subject was dropped. Yet there were times when I think the past must have been in both our hearts; times when we lingered side by side under the gray walls, keeping silence as we paced up and down. But the early blossoms of spring, and the drifting leaves of autumn, spake to each of us in the same eternal language. "I am the Resurrection and the Life, saith the Lord; he that believeth in Me, though he were dead, yet shall he live; and he that liveth and believeth in Me shall never die."

The day came when I repeated my last lesson to Mrs. Redmond; and during that Easter vacation Aunt Esther and I worked hard at the dresses I was to take with me to boarding-school. They were plain and simple frocks, made of inexpensive materials, but in those days I was abundantly contented with them. I shed many tears at the thought of leaving Prior's Row, and breaking the old home ties; and Aunt Esther, although she tried to comfort me, cried too.

"Well, never mind, Aunty," I said, suddenly brightening up. "I shall earn money as a governess by-and-by; and then Daddy shall live in ease and comfort. I'm going to save it all for him."

Ida Sedgeworth and I were still destined to be schoolfellows. I think some distant relation must have assisted her father to send her to St. Agatha's College, and she was delighted at the prospect of the change.

"I'm glad I'm going to a real ladies' school," said she. "I shall be in my proper place there, 'in my element,' as papa says. Blanch Lincoln has been there for a year—how surprised she will be to see us!"

"Mrs. Cravenhurst did not tell me much about my school-mates," said I, musingly.

"Don't you know that the Bishop's daughters are among the pupils?" asked Ida. "And Lady Eva, and Lady Marion Chester, too?"

"I am almost surprised that Mrs. Sanby consents to receive me at the College," I remarked.

"Well I don't suppose she would have done so if it hadn't been to oblige the Dean's wife," rejoined my friend candidly. "I've heard papa say that Mrs.

"I did my best to be perfectly composed."

Cravenhurst is the most popular lady in the county. Everybody does as *she* likes."

Easter passed quickly away; and one April morning, betwixt sunshine and showers, the Dean's carriage rolled along the High Street, conveying me to my destination. Mrs. Cravenhurst never did anything by halves, and having detected in me a slight dread lest my new associates should regard me with scorn, she decided to take me to the school herself.

The College was a heavy gray mansion, almost as old as the cathedral itself. Its walls had once sheltered a community of nuns, and there was still an air of cloistered seclusion about the place. We drove up a long avenue of chestnuts, and stopped before the hall door, while I did my best to be perfectly composed.

But later, when the sound of the carriage wheels died away on the gravel, and I was left alone amongst strangers, my heart felt very desolate indeed. An English teacher took me upstairs to my chamber, a large airy room, containing four small bedsteads, ranged at intervals along the walls. There were two toilet tables with full-sized dressing-glasses, and four little circular washing-stands. My bed was pointed out to me, my box stood beside it; and I was shown a chest of drawers, which I was to share with another girl. Ida Sedgeworth made her appearance soon after my arrival, and we found with great satisfaction that we were to be room-mates.

I soon became accustomed to my new life, and set to work with all my might to make the most of its advantages. With my schoolfellows I was on very good terms, although Ida was my only intimate friend. In fact she was so exacting, and contrived so completely to absorb my spare time, that I had small chance of taking another companion.

"What makes you so fond of Ida Sedgeworth?" asked Kate Brandon one day. She was the Bishop's eldest daughter, a quiet observing girl, and a universal favourite.

"I can scarcely tell you," I answered. "One can't always account for likings and dislikings. But perhaps it may be because Ida is delicate and rather helpless."

"Do you think she really loves you for your own sake?"

"I don't quite understand," said I, in a puzzled tone.

"If she had no longer any need of your aid, if, in short, she could do without you, do you believe she would cling to you as she does now?"

"I think so; I hope so," I replied hurriedly, for the words had given me a sharp pang.

I did not continue the conversation, but ran off to seek Ida, and reassure myself of her affection for me. It was the recreation hour; she had complained of headache during the classes, and would probably be lying down in her bedroom. Thither I repaired, and found her just awaking from a doze. She seemed languidly pleased at my coming, and I took a seat by her side.

"Is your head better, dear?" I inquired.

"Yes, thanks; but it still throbs very much. I wish you had some eau-de-Cologne, Bessie."

"I have only a bottle of smelling salts. Shall I fetch it for you?"

"Yes; and then tell me a story, or read to me. I want to be amused."

I brought her the salts, shook up her pillow, and obediently began an extemporized tale. But Kate Brandon's words clung to me like burrs, and were not to be easily shaken off. I wandered in my narrative, and finally lost the thread altogether.

"What ails you, Bessie?" asked Ida, raising herself on her elbow to look at me.

"Nothing," I said quickly, but my eyes were filled with tears.

"Have you been getting into a scrape?" was her next query.

"No dear; I am feeling a little foolish, that's all."

"Do you mean that you are home-sick?"

"Not now, although I am sometimes. Ida, I want to ask you a question."

"What is it?" she said in some surprise.

"I want to know if you love me, really and truly?"

"Is that all? Why Bessie, how can you be so absurd? Of course I do."

"And you will never suffer anything to change you?"

"Of course not. What has come to you?" she rejoined, flinging herself back impatiently.

I was not thoroughly satisfied, I had expected some warmer assurance than this.

"I tell you what," said Ida, a few minutes afterwards, "I really hate that Blanch Lincoln. She treats both you and me as if we were inferior beings."

"I don't like her myself," I replied. "I think she is the only girl in the College who has ever shown me unkindness."

The Midsummer holidays came, and I returned to Prior's Row in triumph, bearing sundry certificates of merit, and was received with joyful welcome.

CHAPTER VI.

Change.

ONE August day, when the heat had been unusually oppressive, we all hailed the termination of the morning study hours with heartfelt delight. Thoroughly tired in body and mind, I went up to my room to wash my face and hands. The large cool apartment was deliciously fresh after the heated schoolroom, and I sat down by the open window with a sigh of relief.

"I'm glad you are come, Bessie," said Ida's voice. She was at the farther end of the chamber, and I had not observed her.

"I am thankful the morning's work is over," I answered wearily.

"I'm glad you are come," she repeated, "because I want you to brush my hair for me. I'm too tired and hot to do it myself."

"O Ida!" I said gently, "I feel quite spent. And you had some of your lessons excused, and left the schoolroom before I did."

"Now Bessie, that isn't like you. I am more delicate than any one in the College, and you don't pity me a bit. O dear, I wish I had Nurse Murray here! She would brush my hair without any fuss. Everybody in this place is so selfish."

"Very well," I said resignedly, "I will do it, Ida."

She placed herself in a chair before the toilet-table, while I, standing behind her, untwisted the coil of light-brown hair to arrange it afresh. I remember to this day the reflection of our two faces in the looking-glass, and the deadly pallor fast overspreading my own. The voices of the girls in the garden below drifted in through the open window, and across the level green meadows I could see the beautiful old minster. My back ached, my arms and hands grew utterly weary, and I was sick and faint, but Ida sat on, complacently enjoying the sensation of being gently brushed and combed.

"Don't hurry over it Bessie," said she. "It's so nice."

As she spoke there was a tap at the door, and one of the maids looked in.

"If you please, Miss Sedgeworth, your papa has called to see you," she said, and went away.

"Ah, then you must just coil my hair up at once," observed Ida, yawning.

I obeyed in silence, with trembling fingers which had scarcely power to complete their task. Ida rose from her seat, cast a hasty glance at herself, and hurried off; while I, sinking into the chair she had just quitted, lost all consciousness.

I was restored to my senses by feeling a dash of cold water against my face. I opened my eyes, and the various objects in the room appeared to be spinning round and round.

"Where am I? What's the matter?" I asked.

"You have had a fainting-fit my dear," replied Miss Maitland, the junior English teacher, who was bending over me; "but you'll soon be better."

Kate Brandon entered with a flask of eau-de-Cologne, and began to bathe my temples, and then they helped me to reach my bed.

"Carrie Ainslie came in here about fifteen minutes ago," explained Miss Maitland, "and she found you had fainted in your chair. She was frightened, and called me."

"I can't remember anything after Ida left the room," said I, languidly. "I had been brushing her hair, I think I felt very tired and sick."

"Had you been standing up to perform the office of lady's-maid to Miss Sedgeworth?" inquired Miss Maitland, significantly.

"Yes."

"You ought to have been taking rest," said the teacher. "Another time, my dear, you must let Miss Sedgeworth brush her hair for herself."

By-and-by they left me, and I lay dreamily listening for Ida's footstep; but it came not. Presently some one entered softly, and I looked up with an expectant smile; but it was only Carrie Ainslie, good-naturedly bringing me a cup of tea.

"I've a grand piece of news to tell; are you strong enough to hear it?" said she.

"Oh yes; what is it?"

"Well; Ida Sedgeworth's father has become a rich man. His eldest brother was drowned yesterday by the upsetting of a boat, and Ida's three little cousins perished at the same time; so Ida is a great heiress."

"Ida an heiress!" I repeated. "But what a sad thing. Isn't she very sorry for her uncle and his children?"

"She doesn't appear to be overwhelmed with grief," rejoined my informant, drily.

"Does she know that I am ill?" I asked eagerly.

"Yes."

My head sunk back on the pillow, and I burst into tears.

"Don't cry about her," said Carrie, kissing me. "She isn't worth it. Drink your tea, there's a dear."

I thanked her, and composed myself; but I was too sorely hurt to eat or drink just then. Afterwards, when the twilight began to steal over the room, I undressed, feebly enough, and retired to rest. But Ida never came to inquire for me.

I awoke next morning with sensations of weakness and languor. The other girls had already left the chamber, for the prayer-bell was ringing loudly. Presently, one of the maids brought my breakfast, with a kind message from Mrs. Sanby, desiring me not to rise until I felt strong.

A little later I went down into the schoolroom, and contrived to toil through my lessons, although my head ached wearily, and my heart was as heavy as lead. We were set free for the rest of the day, as it was Saturday, and when our early dinner was over, I fetched my broad-brimmed hat and crept out into a sheltered part of the grounds, feeling too feeble to join my companions. There was a favourite spot of mine under the boughs of an old pear-tree, and thither I repaired, taking my seat upon the grass, close to the gray, crumbling wall of the garden. The indefinite leafy murmur, and the soft summer air, soothed and lulled me until I fell into a doze, leaning my head against the stem of the tree.

But I did not sleep profoundly, for ere long I became conscious, in a dreamy way, of the sound of voices coming nearer and nearer to my retreat. And then, while still only half aroused, I heard Blanch Lincoln speaking.

"It was a fortunate accident for you, Ida," said she. "Have you heard particulars?"

"A letter came to me this morning from papa," answered Ida, "inclosing one from Uncle Michael's solicitor."

"And how did the affair happen?"

"Just through my uncle's own carelessness. He was staying with his three children at an out-of-the-way place in the Highlands. They wanted to cross a loch to reach the little island where they intended to picnic. And then, somehow, owing to Uncle Michael's mismanagement, the boat was upset, and they were all drowned."

"You'll have to get your mourning, Ida," said Blanch. "Shall I go with you to Blakeley's and help you select your black dresses?"

"Thank you," was the ready answer. "I shall be glad of your aid, I have so few friends."

"You must beware of low companions," continued Blanch, oracularly. "If you want to cultivate good society, avoid all friendships with your inferiors. You really will have to drop that little Bessie Mere."

"She has been good-natured," rejoined Ida, hesitating; "and she may perhaps fancy that she has some claim on me; but——"

"There's no fear of that, Ida Sedgeworth," cried I, suddenly starting up and facing the astonished pair. I was wide awake now, and burning with indignation.

"Dear me, Bessie, how you startled me!" exclaimed Ida. "I thought you were in your own room."

"Aren't you ashamed of playing eavesdropper!" asked Blanch, angrily.

But I did not deign to notice her words. My gaze was fixed on Ida's face, looking piercingly into those wandering eyes that shrank from meeting mine.

"Do you think," I said, more calmly, "do you think I would fasten any claim upon you because I have been your friend? Don't you know me better than that, Ida? Don't you know that it was your poverty and weakness which first made me cling to you and love you?"

"Noble sentiments," sneered Blanch.

But my words remained unanswered. Pulling her companion's arm, Ida whispered, "Come away," and they left me to myself.

The shrubbery hid the last flutter of their muslin dresses, and the sound of their footsteps ceased. I waited until they were out of hearing, and then, with a low passionate wail, I flung myself prostrate on the grass. It was the first great heart wound—the first snapping of a broken reed—and it pierced me deeply and sorely.

I rose slowly at last, worn out and spent, and stood leaning against the tree. Then, with a curious calmness, I began to probe this wound of mine, to know how deep it was. I had loved this girl dearly, and I had suddenly found out that she had never been worth loving at all.

It was well for me at that moment that I remembered all the good people I had ever known. There were my father and Aunt Esther; there were Mrs. Cravenhurst and the Dean; the world was not made up of Ida Sedgeworths and Blanch Lincolns. And yet—and yet—my grief was hard to bear.

CHAPTER VII.

Christmas.

Weeks passed on, and at Michaelmas it was generally known that Ida intended to leave the College at Christmas. But in the meanwhile she shunned me in every possible way, keeping close to Blanch Lincoln, and never exchanging a sentence with me if she could avoid it. At first this state of affairs cost me much pain, and I felt lonely and desolate. Yet as time went by, and I saw more and more plainly how unwise I had been in my choice of a friend, I ceased to regret her conduct. I even found out that it was pleasant to have my leisure hours to myself, to be set free from her unreasonable demands and exactions. And it was a relief when she finally obtained leave to change her room, for the chamber occupied by Blanch. She lost no time in replenishing her scanty wardrobe. Rich and costly dresses, made and trimmed in the latest fashion, took the place of her former shabby garments. Her manner, too, improved; she was less touchy and fretful, and she grew a little more popular with her schoolfellows.

The important day came when all the good marks were reckoned up, and then it was found that I was entitled to the first prize. It was no small disappointment to some of the elder girls to lose what they, too, had toiled hard to win; yet no one seemed mortified at my success, saving Blanch Lincoln. As I passed her, carrying the beautifully bound volume in my hand, she muttered audibly: "How stupid of Mrs. Sanby to give her a book for a prize; she must be sick of the sight of books; the little shop in Prior's Row is crammed with them." This remark was addressed to Ida, who answered it with a sneering smile.

Then came the usual clatter and bustle incidental to the "breaking-up." Servants hurried to and fro, sundry articles were lost and found, little quarrels were made up, little presents were exchanged, boxes were packed and corded, and kisses were given and received. But no word of farewell was spoken by Ida to me. I was on my knees upon the floor of my bedroom turning the key of my trunk, when she entered the chamber equipped for departure. She had come in search of Carrie Ainslie, of whom she had borrowed a pencil.

"Here's the pencil, Carrie," said she. "Thank you very much; and good-bye."

She held out her hand, delicately gloved in gray kid, and lifted her face to give a parting kiss.

"Good-bye," rejoined Carrie, rather carelessly returning the salute.

I rose to my feet and stepped quickly forwards.

At that last moment I was willing to let all the old grievances be forgotten for the sake of the old love.

"Good-bye, Ida," I said. "I hope you will be very happy."

A slight flush crossed her face; she drew back, and bowing coldly, quitted the room without another word.

"There goes a mean-spirited girl!" exclaimed Carrie, as the silk skirts rustled away through the corridor. "And I, for one, don't wish her back again."

I drew my breath quickly to keep down a sob, and applied myself once more to the key of my box.

Prior's Row looked darker and dingier than ever, in the twilight of that winter afternoon, when I trod the narrow causeway, carrying a large brown paper parcel under my arm. But the sunshine within me put all external gloom to flight, and when I reached the well-known doorway, I had forgotten all the dignity of my sixteen years. With a childish hop, skip, and jump, I crossed the threshold, and rushed into my father's arms, covering his face with kisses.

"Daddy, daddy! I've won the prize!" I shouted. "Won't aunty be proud of me now?"

"Bless you my darling," cried Aunt Esther, stepping out of the little parlour. "What a good girl you are! and how hard you must have worked!"

"But she isn't thinner, is she?" said my father, anxiously regarding me. "She hasn't hurt herself with over-study?"

"O no, no!" I answered, joyously. "I'm quite well, and so glad to be at home again."

The Visit to the Deanery.

I went upstairs to my little garret, which seemed all the smaller after my spacious chamber at the College, and peeped out at the darkening sky. Down below me, and all around, lay the house-roofs and chimneys, and the smoky tiles whereon the cats prowled noiselessly, watching for unwary sparrows. It was all unchanged; looking on these familiar objects, I could scarcely realize that my childhood had gone by, like a tale that is told, leaving me standing on the verge of womanhood.

It was a happy little group that gathered at the tea-table that night. Here there were no concealments. I was free to pour out all the story of Ida's fickleness and unworthiness; free to confess the pain I had felt.

"It *is* hard, isn't it, daddy?" said I, laying my hand on his. "It makes one feel half sorry that one has a loving heart."

"No, no," he answered, quickly. "Not that. Christ's heart was the most loving heart in all the world, Bessie; and are we ever pierced and wounded as He was? Better a thousand times to love and be betrayed, than to be incapable of loving!"

"Well, well," said Aunt Esther, impatiently, "it would be a good thing if some folks had windows in their breasts, that we might look into them, to see if they were to be trusted, before we began to love them. What a deal of trouble it would save."

My father smiled at this, but shook his head, as if he did not quite agree with it.

On the following morning I went to pay a visit to

the Deanery, to show my prize to Mrs. Cravenhurst. It was a cheery winter day. The beautiful windows glittered bright in the sun; while here and there the ivy showed its rich dark green. Within the Deanery all was bustle and pleasant preparation. There was roast beef to be cooked for the poor, and there were puddings to be made for hungry children; a kind of business which seemed to give Mrs. Cravenhurst great satisfaction; but she found leisure to bestow a hearty greeting, and rejoice with me over my success.

Then came Christmas-day, and the bells clashed out a joyous peal. Wreaths of holly and ivy were twined about the massive pillars of the great minster, and the stalls of carved oak were adorned with evergreens. The choir sang " Unto us a Child is born; unto us a Son is given! and the government shall be upon His shoulders, and His name shall be called Wonderful, Counsellor, the Mighty God, the Everlasting Father, the Prince of Peace."

" The Prince of Peace; ay, that's the sweetest name of all," said my father, as we walked homewards arm-in-arm.

" I think it is," I answered, musingly.

" Yes; it comes so sweetly after all the other grander names. Without Him, Bessie, we should never know what Peace is."

I looked up at the dear face by my side, and pressed his arm without speaking. I was very happy; but the grand music, and the solemn thoughts, had brought tears into my eyes.

CHAPTER VIII.

My New Life Begins.

ONE more year was spent at the college—the happiest year of my whole school life. Free from the restraint of Ida's presence, I entered more fully into the pursuits of my companions, making myself useful to them in many ways. And while I was adding to my stock of learning—laying up the honey of knowledge for future use—Ida was revelling in those very pleasures for which she had been wont to pine, and leading her father captive to her will.

Many well-meaning people had pointed out to Mr. Sedgeworth the folly of permitting so young a girl to enter society before her education was completed; but their arguments were utterly thrown away. He confessed that his daughter's life was not in accordance with his wishes; she had, he admitted, got beyond his control.

My last day at the College came—a day of leave-takings, kisses and tears. My schoolmates gathered round me with eager expressions of goodwill, and even Mrs. Sanby unbent her dignity to give me a hearty embrace. I returned to Prior's Row, again bearing with me the prize; but carrying a heavier heart this time, and walking with a slower step, for I knew that in a few short weeks I should say a long good-bye to my dear old home. True to her promise of looking after my interests, Mrs. Cravenhurst had already obtained for me a suitable situation.

"Don't fret, Bessie," whispered my father, as I laid my head on his shoulder and sobbed. "The Dean's lady—God bless her—has been here, telling me all about your new home. And you're sure to be happy my girl; you'll have every luxury that heart can wish. You know, Bessie" (here the whisper grew lower still) "you wouldn't find the old bookshop quite to your liking now. You've been used to better food and finer ways—and, and—you're a real lady, you are indeed!"

"No, no," I burst out, impetuously. "I'm only your own little Bessie!"

Nevertheless I had to get reconciled to the idea of leaving Priorsbury, and my benefactress comforted me in her wonted kindly fashion. She had arranged for me to undertake the education of a little girl in delicate health, the daughter of a widow lady well known to the Dean.

I pass over the bitterness of parting from my home. I will go on at once to that bleak January day when I found myself at Euston Square railway station, standing disconsolately before a blazing fire in the waiting-room. Mrs. Daverill's man-servant was gone to look after my luggage, while I shivered, and wondered what Mrs. Daverill herself was like. I had passed the greater part of the journey in tears: what would she say to my woe-begone aspect?

A few minutes later, and I was rattling along the crowded thoroughfares in a cab, the servant having taken his seat on the box with the driver. From time to time I caught in the shop window panes, a reflection of my trunk perched unsteadily on the roof of the vehicle, and swaying to and fro in an alarming manner. It contained all my earthly belongings, and I was harassed with dire misgivings as to its safety. But to my unspeakable relief, the jolting and racketing soon came to an end, and I was duly deposited at Mrs. Daverill's door.

Later still my fears had all subsided, and my pupil and I were taking tea together in our comfortable little schoolroom. Rosa was gentle and timid, and very pretty; but although nearly fourteen years of age, she was backward in her studies. Her health had always been delicate, and during her papa's long illness she had been left a good deal to herself. She was sent to bed at an early hour, and after she was gone, her mother entered the room and settled herself by the fireside, prepared for a long chat.

I had not expected the friendly reception I met with from Mrs. Daverill. Her bright, genial manner took me by surprise, and won my heart at once.

She was a handsome, portly woman of four or five and forty, still wearing her mourning, with a modified widow's cap, and her rich sable draperies became her very well.

"And how is my good friend Dean Cravenhurst?" she asked, when the plans for her daughter's education had been duly discussed.

It was pleasant to hear the familiar name, and I answered brightly that he was well.

"And his pretty wife?" she continued. "You are a great favourite of hers, I find: 'her pet,' as she calls you in her letters. What an odd thing that the Dean should marry Clara Severn. She was a mere school-girl when I saw her last—a sweet little creature even in those days. Afterwards she became engaged to her cousin, Hugh Ashburn, the son of her mother's sister. Ah, poor fellow! I knew him very well indeed."

I longed to hear more of poor Jack's beloved master, and my heart throbbed quickly, but I did not venture to ask questions. However, Mrs. Daverill was disposed to talk, and she rambled on.

"Poor dear Hugh! he was absolutely devoted to Clara, and somehow they seemed made for each other. But they could not afford to marry; Hugh had nothing besides his pay, and although he longed to take Clara away from her uncomfortable home at her uncle's, he was obliged to wait his time. Ah, the time never came! Hugh fell fighting at the battle of Inkermann, and there is Clara quietly settled down as Mrs. Cravenhurst. It is a matter-of-fact ending to a romantic story; isn't it, Miss Mere?"

But I could not speak; my eyes were full of tears.

"I see you have a tender heart," said Mrs. Daverill half smiling. "You haven't been knocked about in the world and hardened yet. And these Cravenhursts are dear friends of yours; well, they are good people. I am very glad that Clara is safely provided for; she had a hard time of it in her uncle's house. The Reverend Charles Severn was the most disagreeable man I ever met, and his daughters were jealous of their cousin's beauty. And Clara behaved very well when the Dean asked her to marry him. She told him all the story of her former love affair, and asked him if he could be content to take a woman whose heart was in her lover's grave. Wasn't that a poetical speech?" added the speaker, with a soft little laugh.

"The Dean is a wise man," she went on, "and he understood all that sort of thing. So they were married; he makes her a good husband, and she makes him a good wife. How did you first become acquainted with her, Miss Mere?"

I related the old story of the ruby ring, carefully suppressing all the pathetic details, and allowing Mrs. Daverill to believe that my benefactress was actuated merely by a sudden liking for myself. She heard me throughout with evident interest, and when I had finished, again referred to the manner in which the Dean and his wife had spoken of me.

"So you see I am prepared to like you very much, and to receive you as the friend of my friends," she said, with a pleasant smile, as she wished me good-night.

I went to bed no little pleased with my reception. Mrs. Cravenhurst's favour had smoothed the way for my feet. Better would it have been for me, perhaps, if I had been received in a more ordinary manner; but there were many lessons for me to learn—lessons which could only be taught me through humiliation and sorrow.

Rosa Daverill and I speedily began to understand each other. Her shyness, and a certain irritability of disposition, had given her mother the impression that her daughter was a "very odd little girl—quite unlike other folk's children."

"Try and make her more lively and sociable," Mrs. Daverill said to me. "It vexes me to see her sit still like a little mumchance, when people are all talking around her. I don't like your very quiet girls—they look as if they were always plotting mischief."

My youth and good spirits soon set Rosa at her ease with me, and I became her companion as well as her instructress. But in the meanwhile I could not yet forget all that was left behind in Priorsbury, and many were the loving thoughts and fond letters I sent to the dear ones far away. How long should I keep "unspotted from the world"?

CHAPTER IX.

MY NEW LIFE.

THE bleak winter days glided away; but long before the few trees in Clayton Square were dotted with tiny green buds, I had grown well contented with my new lot. Mrs. Daverill sought my company frequently, and delighted especially in my singing.

"You are a real treasure to me, Miss Mere," she would say; "I am getting sadly old and bored and world-worn. And you are so fresh and young and bright. Didn't Mrs. Cravenhurst tell you that you had a lovely voice, child?"

"She used to like to hear me sing," I replied; for in truth Mrs. Cravenhurst, although she had been wont to encourage me, never praised me so broadly as Mrs. Daverill was doing.

Yet want of sincerity could not be laid to Mrs. Daverill's charge. She was easy-tempered and somewhat frivolous, enjoying the passing hour's gratification much as a butterfly might have done. She had a way of saying almost everything that came into her head; but to do her justice, these thoughtless remarks were never malicious or impertinent.

March and April passed by and May set in. By this time I was beginning to revel in my new life, and to have a very exalted opinion of my own powers. Mrs. Daverill held me up to her friends as quite a prodigy, never failing to speak of me as the pet and protégée of Mrs. Cravenhurst, the wife of the Dean of Priorsbury. It was delightful to find oneself flattered and caressed on all sides, when one had looked forward to occupying a far less pleasant position. I began unconsciously to regard my talents and accomplishments in a new light, and to consider Bessie Mere a very superior person indeed.

We took long drives in an open carriage, country drives as Mrs. Daverill called them, through green lanes and past suburban villas, where the gardens bloomed with lilacs and laburnums; but it did not seem to me like the 'real country.' There was nothing rural about it, I asserted; there were no sequestered spots, no untrodden ways. Woods and parks were common property, and there was not a single shady haunt that had not been trampled over and over by 'holiday-making Cockneys.'

"Why Miss Mere," said Rosa, who could say sharp things occasionally, "I heard you talking the other day about 'the rights of the people,' and I thought you liked them to be happy and enjoy themselves! Would you wish to keep the poor hard-worked Londoners away from these pleasant places, just because they destroy the privacy and seclusion?"

It was a long speech for a girl of fourteen to make, and it showed that if Rosa was not very advanced in her studies, she was far from being deficient in powers of observation. Her words brought the colour into my cheeks, and I remembered who and what I was.

"You have made me ashamed of myself, Rosa," I said smiling. "It is a selfish love of Nature which wants to keep her beauties from the multitude; and these poor Londoners,—I was forgetting how precious the green grass and leafy trees are to them."

Even while I spoke I recollected my own childish delight in the smooth turf and the flowers under the cathedral walls, when I could escape from the gloom of Prior's Row. I was the daughter of a poor man: how dared I murmur if other poor men's children sought the fresh air and the pleasant places within their reach as eagerly as I did?

I felt humbled in my own estimation, and determined that on my return to Clayton Square I would write a long letter to my father, telling him that I feared his little Bessie was growing proud and selfish, and stood in need of a word or two of his wise counsel. But this letter was destined never to be written, for other events occurred to put it quite out of my mind.

On that very evening Mrs. Daverill gave a dinner-party, and I was desired to make my appearance with Rosa in the drawing-room, to sing several favourite songs. I went upstairs to my room, with my head full of my toilette; and I could not help regretting my lack of ornaments. Fortunately however, there was one dress in my wardrobe which I had never worn: a

F

dress of delicate, white India muslin, given me by Mrs. Cravenhurst before I left Priorsbury.

"You may find it useful, Bessie," she had said; "and I don't think I shall ever wear white again."

Aunt Esther had got it up in her best style, and had praised the fineness of the texture very highly. I took it down from its peg, and was shaking out its soft folds, when Gregson knocked at the door.

"Come in," I said.

"Can I help you, miss?" she asked: "I've just dressed Miss Rosa."

I gladly accepted her services, and saw with secret satisfaction that the sight of the white robe inspired her with increased respect for its owner. She examined the costly lace with which it was trimmed, and ventured openly to express her admiration. Then I sat down in front of the looking-glass before the open window, while she braided my thick brown hair. It was a sweet May evening; the sky was fair and calm, with that transparent clearness which invites the eye to penetrate its depths. The trees in the square were still freshly green, all untouched as yet by the heat and dust of summer, and occasionally a light wind sighed softly through the young leaves. The endless roar of the great city had grown familiar to me now; I had ceased to pine for the quiet of Priorsbury and the sound of the old minster-bells.

My toilette was completed at last, and Gregson regarded her handiwork with no small pride. Her practised fingers had woven my hair into a regal coronet of braids at the back of my head, while over my temples it was suffered to wave and ripple as Nature willed. I wore a belt of cerise ribbon, and a breast-knot of the same hue. The looking-glass showed me a small brown face, with round dimpled cheeks just touched with carmine, and large dark eyes with black lashes and eyebrows; a little cherry mouth and a nose whose tendency to turn up was a sore annoyance to its possessor. I smiled, not ill-pleased with the figure I saw there, and tripped downstairs with a light heart.

I sang my best that night, and was duly applauded and caressed. Before the company took their departure, Mrs. Daverill had been easily persuaded to let me sing at a private amateur concert, which was to be held in the drawing-room of one of her friends. It was for a charitable purpose I was told, and I felt myself glowing with pleasure. It was so pleasant to assist in a good work, and gratify one's own vanity at the same time. I returned to my chamber happy and excited. The moonlight shone fully into the room, and one long white ray fell across my blotting-book, which lay open upon the table. It reminded me of the letter to my father, the letter that ought to have been written and was not.

I sat down and hastily scrawled a few lines, ready for the morning's post. My conscience told me that he would expect more than this from his child, but I began to make excuse. I was tired, my engagements were very numerous, and Prior's Row and the little bookshop were miles away from me.

And on the morrow I was full of selfish schemes.

My salary was a liberal one, and it had at first appeared more than sufficient for my wants. But now I found out that it was not inexhaustible, for my requirements were increasing fast.

Where was the little Bessie Mere who had once trodden the stone-paved alley by the prebendaries' houses, with such shabby boots, and such a dingy frock? Where was the simple, hard-working schoolgirl, who was thankful to wear a plain dress that was whole and neat? And where was the loving, warm-hearted daughter, who had indulged such fond dreams of saving her money for her father's sake?

CHAPTER X.

LIVING FOR SELF.

THERE seemed to be quite a rage just then among Mrs. Daverill's friends, for amateur concerts. My services were constantly required, and I was praised and flattered far more than I deserved. The India muslin did duty again and again; but there were gloves, and knicknacks, and flowers to be purchased, and my money melted like snow before the sun. I gave few thoughts to my home during those brief summer days. I no longer cared to call up the aspect of the little room wherein my vacant place was kept sacred, and where my brief hurried letters were read again and again. I forgot the gray walls tapestried with lichen and ivy, and the tall spire ever pointing upwards to the bright heaven. Even Mrs. Cravenhurst's gentle words of counsel began to fade out of my remembrance, although her name was often on my lips. And—saddest, darkest sign of all—I ceased to cry unto Him who was the guide of my youth—ceased to think about that Friend who sticketh closer than a brother.

My life just then was like the weather, all glaring sultry sunshine by day, and hot steamy vapours by night. Slowly but surely, noxious insects were creeping over the field where the good grain had sprung up, and threatening the growing crops with destruction. Selfishness, vanity, and pride were blighting the green ears. Ah me! it needed a storm to clear the air and kill the vermin; it needed showers of passionate tears to soften the hard dry ground.

In August Mrs. Daverill prepared to leave London. Rosa was pining for fresh air, and she herself was jaded and worn with excitement and late hours.

"Where are we going, mamma?" asked my pupil. "I hope you have decided on the seaside."

"I have taken a villa in Ryde," replied Mrs. Daverill. "We shall be amongst our own set there; and the sea breezes will bring the colour back into our cheeks."

I was full of delight and exultation at the new pleasures in store for me; and no little labour was expended on the dresses I deemed necessary for a fashionable watering-place. I sat up far into the nights, sewing and trimming, and rearranging my costumes with unflagging industry; building castles in the air all the while, castles in which self reigned like a queen, and from which all the old innocent hopes and desires were excluded. My labours were completed by the time of our starting from Clayton Square, and I was well pleased to find myself lounging on the cushions of a first-class carriage with Mrs. Daverill and Rosa. Fortunately however, I had sense enough remaining to me to eschew all fine-lady airs, and to be natural in look and manner, but that is all I can say in my own favour.

Our villa in Ryde was delightfully situated; and the back drawing-room, whose windows overlooked the sea, was devoted to the use of my pupil and myself. It was pleasant to feel the fresh salt breeze against my cheek, as I sat at the piano practising my favourite songs; and it was pleasanter still to know that in the neighbouring garden, only separated from ours by a low wall, there were groups of fashionable ladies and idle gentlemen listening to my voice.

Land picnics and water picnics followed each other in rapid succession; and there were parties at home of a less conventional kind than those at Clayton Square. My songs seemed now to be in greater request than ever, and gratified vanity had reached its height—as it generally does before a fall comes. And my fall was not far off.

On a certain Sunday morning I returned from church with Rosa, in high spirits as usual, thinking very little about the service in which I had taken an outward part. For the congregation was a large one, and many of the queens of fashion had been present; while I, instead of entering heart and soul into the worship of God, was glancing furtively hither and thither—getting hints for future self-adornment from their costly toilettes. Mrs. Daverill had remained in the house, and we found her with an open letter in her hand.

"My friend Mrs. Burleigh comes to stay with

me to-morrow," said she. "And she intends bringing with her a young lady who is left in her charge."

The visitors arrived at four o'clock on Monday afternoon, when Rosa and I were sitting quietly at our work in our own sanctum. We heard the carriage stop before the hall-door, and then Mrs. Daverill's voice welcoming her guests. I was acquainted with Mrs. Burleigh's tones, and could hear them distinctly enough, for our door stood ajar; but another person was speaking in a soft plaintive key, which seemed to thrill me with a strange sense of familiarity. Instinctively I dropped my work and listened.

"Rosa," I asked, suddenly; "did you hear the name of the young lady who is under Mrs. Burleigh's care?"

"I think I did, Miss Mere. Oh yes—I remember —it was Sedgeworth."

The colour rushed into my face in a moment. No other person in the world could be so unwelcome to me as Ida; and yet we were under the same roof, and our meeting could not be avoided.

The only thing to be done was to make the best of it, and this I resolved to do. And it was not without a feeling of secret satisfaction that I pictured my quondam friend's astonishment at seeing the changes that time and circumstances had wrought in me. Full of these thoughts, I dressed myself as becomingly as possible, and entered the drawing-room with Rosa as usual.

Ida crimsoned and started visibly when her eyes

met mine; whereas I, being prepared for the encounter, was quite composed. She inclined her head stiffly when I was presented to her by Mrs. Daverill, and I made no reference to our former acquaintance. Then other guests made their appearance, and I was soon called upon for a song.

I complied readily enough, and was repaid by the customary applause. Ida had never possessed any musical talent, and I could see that she writhed under her own sense of inferiority. During that evening she sat sullenly in the shade, and my short-lived triumph was complete.

Days went on, and Miss Sedgeworth's apparent sweetness and gentleness began to win upon Mrs. Daverill, who was good-natured and easily pleased. She tried hard to ingratiate herself with my pupil also, but Rosa did not respond to these advances. Her quick perceptions told her that Ida's manner was artificial; and she owned frankly to me that "she did not like her." In the meanwhile, rumours of the heiress's wealth soon spread through the fashionable circles of Ryde, old acquaintances were renewed, and new ones formed, and she was fêted and caressed on all sides. But I was to her as Mordecai to Haman, and I had a silent satisfaction in provoking the jealousy which I read in every line of her fair face.

It was not long before I found myself brought into contact with another of my old schoolfellows. A fresh bevy of visitors arrived at the villa next door to Mrs. Daverill's; and amongst them were

Blanch Lincoln and her brother. The brother I had never seen before, but his appearance did not impress me favourably; and without knowing why, I instinctively shunned him. Blanch was little altered since her school-days—the same tall, showy blonde, with the same imperious manner—vividly reminding me of the old times at St. Agatha's College.

She was still the obsequious, devoted friend of Ida, and had plainly set her heart upon marrying the heiress to her brother George. Mrs. Daverill thought the Lincolns 'charming young people,' and they visited at her house nearly every day. Both girls treated me with a haughty reserve which I repaid with the composure of indifference.

CHAPTER XI.

Dark Clouds.

I still wrote at intervals to Prior's Row, and to the Deanery, and received ready replies. But my friends knew little of the sort of life I was leading. They believed me to be simply doing my duty in a quiet contented way; never dreaming of the snares and temptations wherewith I was beset; never guessing how completely the love of the world had gained the mastery over my heart. I read their letters often hurriedly and carelessly, for my thoughts were full of other matters. They were all well and happy, I told myself; and my mind was at rest about them. A false security and a fatal rest.

The autumn of that year was one of the mildest and balmiest I have ever known. If the leaves fell and the flowers faded, we heeded them not while the sky was still so calmly bright, and the air soft and sweet. It was about this time that I began to notice a striking change in Ida's manner towards me. She sought my company frequently, talking a little of old times and old friendships, and asking friendly questions about my personal concerns. Her father had gone abroad in delicate health, she told me, and nurse Murray had returned to her Scottish home.

"So you see I am lonely with all my money," she said plaintively. "I was not strong enough to travel with papa—I can't endure the least fatigue. An heiress is not such a happy person as many folks suppose."

When she spoke thus, I felt a faint stirring of my old affection for her, and I did not repel her advances.

"What a beautiful voice you have, Bessie," she remarked one evening, when we were alone together for a few minutes before dinner. She had come noiselessly into the back drawing-room where I was copying music.

"Don't you ever sing now?" I asked.

"Not when you are near," she replied. "I almost envy your gift."

"You cannot envy poor little Bessie Mere?" I said laughing.

"I think I can. By-the-by will you do me a small favour? I want you to write out the words of that song you sang last night."

"O yes; certainly," I rejoined.

"Won't you do it now? Here is a sheet of paper, and your pen and ink are beside you."

She produced some note-paper and laid it on the table before me. As she did so I noticed that her hand trembled.

A little surprised at her eagerness, I wrote out the

"She had come noiselessly into the back drawing-room."

lines from memory, while she stood looking over my shoulder. The ballad consisted only of two verses, and these were soon completed.

"Thank you," she said in a constrained voice.

I looked up, and saw that her face was deadly pale.

"Aren't you well?" I asked quickly.

"O yes; only a little tired after my morning's walk," she answered, and instantly left the room.

Four days passed by without anything of importance taking place. But on the fifth, which was Saturday, I received a note from Mrs. Daverill. Rosa and I were sitting over our tea-table as usual, when Gregson entered and handed me a letter.

"Why, that's mamma's hand-writing," cried Rosa, catching a glimpse of the envelope.

Gregson withdrew, and I opened it at once. It contained only a few words, telling me that for the future my presence would not be required in the drawing-room after dinner; and that Mrs. Daverill requested me from henceforth to remember that I was her daughter's governess, and to order my general conduct with due circumspection.

I dropped the paper on my lap, and sat staring vacantly at my pupil for some seconds. Surprise and indignation utterly overwhelmed me; and my case seemed all the more hopeless because no definite charge was made. I had no chance of defending myself.

"What's the matter, Miss Mere?" asked Rosa anxiously.

"Read this," I said, holding out the letter with trembling fingers.

She ran her eye over its contents, and then it was her turn to gaze blankly at me in unspeakable amazement.

"What does it all mean?" she exclaimed at last. "Surely there is some dreadful mistake!"

"It's a mistake that can't be cleared up," I said, suddenly bursting into tears.

"O, don't cry, don't cry!" pleaded my pupil, flinging her arms round me. "I love you, and I won't see you put upon without cause."

"You can't help it dear," I sobbed.

"Yes I can; I'm going this minute to have it all out with mamma."

"Rosa come back," I entreated. But she had reached the door, and was gone before I could detain her. I scarcely believed that she could do me any good by seeking an interview with her mother, and yet it was some sort of relief to feel that some one was on my side—a feeble ally was better than none. It was a long twenty minutes during which I sat awaiting her return. A breeze sighed through the open window, scattering a few dead leaves and stray petals over my dress, and I shuddered, for it blew with a cold breath upon my cheek. There were slate-coloured clouds gathering in the west, and blotting out the deep pure crimson of the sunset lights—the sea itself looked gray and dreary. I clasped my hands, shivering and listening for Rosa's footstep.

It came at last; but she entered the room slowly, with a dejected face.

"I can't understand it, Miss Mere," she said, taking my cold hands in her own. "Mamma refuses to tell me anything."

"Did she seem to have quite turned against me?" I asked nervously.

"I'll tell you just what passed," replied my pupil, kissing me, "but don't let it distress you too much. I went straight to mamma's dressing-room and opened the door without knocking. She wasn't alone,—Miss Sedgeworth and Miss Lincoln were with her, talking very confidentially. And when Miss Sedgeworth saw me, she said, 'Ah, I expected she would send you.'"

"Go on Rosa," I cried breathlessly; for I felt convinced that my old schoolmates had been devising mischief against me.

"Well, I asked mamma at once why she had written that strange note, and what you had done? And she answered very stiffly, 'I shall not reply to any questions, my dear. I have excellent reasons for wishing Miss Mere to confine herself exclusively to her duties.' Then she shut her lips, and would say no more."

"And Ida and Blanch, did they say nothing?"

"They kept their tongues silent, but they talked with their eyes. Ah, I do believe, Miss Mere, they are at the bottom of it all."

There was company that night; and, sorely against her will, Rosa left me to go into the drawing-room. And I listened to the voices and the music, as I sat solitary in my chamber, with my face hidden in my hands.

A wretched Sunday followed that miserable Saturday evening. Mrs. Daverill avoided me as much as possible, and treated me with formal politeness when I came in her way; and Ida and Mrs. Burleigh took very little notice of me. I should have been quite forlorn but for Rosa, who kept close to my side, striving by a thousand small acts of kindness to give me comfort.

Then came Monday morning; and I was awakened from a troubled slumber by Gregson's knock. She had pushed a letter underneath my door.

I started up; I was feeling less indifferent about home news now—the old ties were tightening again. I sprang out of bed, picked up the letter, and eagerly tore it open. It was in Aunt Esther's handwriting, and ran thus:—

"My dear Child,

"Your father is very ill and longs to see you. Come home to us without delay. God bless you.

"Your loving aunt,

"Esther Mere."

I cried out, a shrill cry that rang through the house. And then in feverish haste I began to seize upon various articles of clothing and heap them into my trunk. What could I do, I asked myself distractedly, to save time?

Of the events that followed, I have no distinct recollection. I can remember that Gregson came and spoke soothingly, packing my box herself. I can recall Rosa's tears and kisses, and something of the aspect of Mrs. Daverill's face, as she bade me good-bye, and put money into my hands. Then there was the journey that seemed interminable—the rush and roar of the train—the strange faces coming and going—and at last the well-known platform at the Priorsbury railway station, and the agony of uncertainty as I reached my home.

"Is he alive, Aunt Esther? Am I too late?"

"He is living dear, and asking for you. Come to him at once."

CHAPTER XII.

"Right dear in the sight of the Lord is the death of
His saints."

I KNEW you'd come to me, Bessie," said my
father softly. "I knew I shouldn't die
without seeing you again."

Before he spoke these words my first
burst of agony was over, and I felt that
we were soon to be parted. I had been
at home for two days, but this was the first time
he had spoken plainly of dying.

"I wish I was going with you, daddy," I answered,
laying my head on his pillow, and trying to keep back
my tears. "You will be far away at rest in the
better country, while I am still here in the midst
of the strife."

"It won't be all strife and sorrow for my little
girl," he said tenderly. "The Lord leads His children through green pastures, and by still waters. He
gives them times of rest and refreshment, and then
they go back stronger to the fight. But is my little
girl really His child?"

"I used to think so, father; but now I am afraid that I have been deceiving myself. I have forgotten Him, and have been so vain and silly and selfish. And when He saw fit to bring a cloud upon my pleasures I was angry and bitter—not sorry that I had gone astray."

"Bessie," said my father, and his voice grew strangely clear as he spoke, "don't you recollect Christian and Hopeful and the other pilgrims? Didn't they often turn out of the narrow way, instead of keeping their faces towards the Celestial City?"

"Yes, daddy. Ah, I used to read about them with you, in the dear old book, when I was a little child."

"And did not God lead them back into the right path again and again? And didn't He bring them safely across the river without a bridge—home to the bright City at last?"

"Yes, yes," I answered sobbing.

"Ay, and I believe He will bring you there too, my child. Even as Christian's children joined him in that home, so you, by God's grace, will join me."

"I think He will, I think He will," I cried, putting my arms about him. "And I will ask Him to lead me always through the Valley of Humiliation —that is the best place for poor proud me."

My father lingered for many days on the margin of that river which 'hath been a terror unto many,' but was no terror to him. To use once more the language of that great writer, whose book he taught me to love, he might truly have said, " I have loved to hear my Lord spoken of, and wherever I have seen the print of His shoe in the earth, there I have coveted to set my foot too." And those few words have told the whole story of his life.

On a Sunday morning, just as the bells were chiming out for service, he crossed the flood—drifting away from us with a calm smile on his face; and we thought that he must have caught sight of the 'shining ones' waiting for him on the other side.

So Aunt Esther and I were left alone in the shabby little house that was so dear to us both; but we did not sorrow wildly, as 'those that have no hope.' Yet I knew, as I knelt down by the side of that quiet grave, that all the brightness of my youth had left me, for who could fill his place? Did I wish him back again? I hope not, I think not; although my tears fell like rain upon the headstone, whereon, by Mrs. Cravenhurst's desire, these words were graven, "Right dear in the sight of the Lord is the death of His saints."

We gave up the shop, and sold our few articles of furniture. But before these last arrangements were completed, I received a letter from Mrs. Daverill, to whom I had written, telling her of my bereavement.

She was deeply grieved to hear of my loss, and she trusted that time would soften my sorrow. There were reasons which would render it unadvisable that I should return to my post; but she wished me to understand that she had a very high opinion of my talents, and was willing to recommend me, if I intended taking another situation.

I carried this unsatisfactory note to Mrs. Cravenhurst and put my cause into her hands. She trusted and believed in me, and she wrote at once to Mrs. Daverill asking for an explanation of her conduct. But no explanation was given, and Mrs. Daverill courteously requested that the subject might be dropped. There were two or three passionately sorrowful letters from Rosa, bewailing her mother's inexplicable behaviour, and stating her belief that Miss Sedgeworth and Miss Lincoln had somehow contrived to make the mischief. These too, I showed to my benefactress, and she professed herself to be of Rosa's opinion.

"I hope we are not misjudging those two girls," she said gravely; "but their characters were not promising in their school-days. Wait patiently, Bessie, the mystery may yet be cleared up."

She spoke of seeking for me another situation among her friends, but with all gratitude and love, I put aside her plan. I should prefer, I said, to become a teacher in a school; I would not risk a return to the life of a private governess. And then Mrs. Sanby, the mistress of St. Agatha's College, came to my aid. She obtained for me the post of second English teacher in a large boarding-school in Clapham, with a salary of thirty-five pounds a year.

I found that Mrs. Daverill at parting with me had paid me more money than was really due; but on my offering to return it she steadfastly refused to take it back. "Rosa owed a great deal to my tuition," she maintained; and "she herself wished me well." So

I kept the sum, and found it useful enough, for our means were very limited.

Just at this time, when Aunt Esther was uncertain what course to take, Mrs. Cravenhurst saw an advertisement in the *Times*, stating that a housekeeper of middle age was required by an elderly gentleman—an invalid. Through her influence my aunt was engaged to fill the place, and to our great joy we found that her employer lived in Clapham.

"God will not leave me desolate," I thought, as once more the train whirled me away from Priorsbury. Aunt Esther's hand was clasping mine, and we sat in silence, looking back at the dear old city we were leaving behind. The mists of the gray November day clouded over the crowd of house-roofs, but the tall spire pierced through the vapours, rising far above them, and catching a gleam of silvery light from a rift in the dull sky. I thought of the little girl who used to look from her garret window in childish wonder at that spire when the heavens were spangled with stars, and the rest of the household were asleep. Where was she now? It almost seemed as if she had been buried in a certain dear grave under the gray walls, and a sad, thoughtful woman was come in her stead.

I pass over my first introduction to Miss Goodwin's school in Clapham; it was like most other establishments of its kind, and I had no difficulty in fitting into my place. My duties now were more onerous; I had little time at my own disposal—little leisure for sitting still to muse over the sorrowful past. Plenty of hard work was the best thing in the world for me, and I did not dislike my lot.

Aunt Esther and I contrived to meet every week; her situation was an easy and comfortable one, and her master was liberal and kind. So the time sped on; the winter passed away and the spring came round again. Then followed a hot, sultry summer; there was much sickness in the neighbourhood, and we had several invalids amongst our boarders. My health, a little enfeebled by past trouble, gave way at last under the strain of nursing and tending our sick pupils, and Aunt Esther entreated me to spend the midsummer holidays in some rural place.

It was by Miss Goodwin's advice that I fixed on the small village of Axwood, in Sussex. It was a spot little frequented by visitors, she told me; and I had a natural dread of meeting any of my former acquaintances. My heart was yet too sore to permit of my going to Priorsbury; it was best to choose a locality wherewith I was entirely unacquainted.

Aunt Esther was unable to accompany me; her master, Mr. Gill, was seriously indisposed, and her services could not be spared. So early on a brilliant July morning, before the intense heat of the day began to be felt, I set off on my journey to Axwood alone.

CHAPTER XIII.

A STRANGE MEETING.

AXWOOD lies in a small green nest, encompassed by richly-wooded hills; a quaint little hamlet with primitive ways of its own, and a good opinion of its sayings and doings. The railroad has not ventured within five miles of it, and it utterly rejects, as far as possible, all modern innovations. My worthy landlady, for example, would have nothing to do with 'new-fangled kitcheners,' but kindled her fire on the open hearth, and smoked her bacon up the wide chimney, as her mother and grandmother had done before her.

"Them plans," she maintained, "always *have* answered very well; and where's the use of alterin' what don't need improvin'?"

I did not argue the point. I liked the place all the better for being behind the times. It was pleasant to leave the great world, that must

> "Spin for ever down the ringing groove of change,"

and rest awhile among a class of people who seemed absolutely to be standing still.

A fortnight passed away, and I was quite at home in the large, rambling old farmhouse, and on the best of terms with its inmates. My health was improving, my letters to Aunt Esther were written in better spirits, and as I sat at my bedroom window one Monday morning, retrimming a shabby dress, I was contented and almost happy. Suddenly the latch of the front gate clicked loudly, and looking up, I saw a stranger of most unwonted aspect coming along the gravel path. Peeping through my screen of vine-leaves, I took note of her fashionable bonnet and little furbelowed parasol, wondering what she could want in such a retired nook as Axwood.

She entered the house, and then there was a sound of much talking below, a confusion of tongues, followed by the tread of feet upon the stairs, and the opening and shutting of doors. By-and-by my landlady knocked for admittance.

"Only to think of it!" said she. "That fly-away madam—did you see her, miss?—was but a lady's maid, and her young lady's a-staying at the Ram. Very discontented with the accommodation there she is, and no wonder. She wants to take lodgings in this very house for her missus, who's terrible sickly, she says. Now what be I to do?"

"Let her come by all means Mrs. Pine," I answered; for I pitied the poor invalid who had taken up her quarters in the slovenly little inn—the only ill-kept house in the village.

The new lodger made her appearance on the same day, walking slowly and feebly, and leaning on her servant's arm. I was still sitting at my vine-wreathed window, and looked out at her with some curiosity as she reached the garden gate. 'Truth is stranger than fiction.' I make no apology for using the oft-quoted adage which darted into my mind at the moment, for there standing before me was the very person whom of all others I least wished to meet—Ida Sedgeworth.

We are apt to be very satirical on novelists for bringing their heroes and heroines together at unlikely times, and in improbable places; and yet our criticism is often unjust. If all the strange meetings and remarkable coincidences of most of our lives were honestly recorded, set down fairly in black and white, we should cease to ridicule the so-called 'extravagances' of story-tellers ancient and modern.

Ida's face, from which her veil was thrown back, was perfectly colourless; its expression that of sore distress. She must be, I felt convinced, in trouble of some serious kind. It was strange for her, the spoiled heiress, to come to this lonely little village, attended only by her maid. I tried however, to be unconcerned about her, and to go on with my sewing as before. But these attempts were useless; I put up my work at last, and sat musing with my hands lying idle in my lap.

Mrs. Pine's heavy footstep broke in upon my reverie. She opened the door—this time without knocking—and entered in considerable trepidation.

"I wish Miss," she began, "you'd come and see that poor young lady. Somehow I don't like her

"The new lodger made her appearance . . . leaning on her servant's arm."

looks. The master and me have always been that hearty, that I ain't well skilled in sickness."

I hesitated, but only for a moment. Rising from my seat, I followed the good woman out into the long uncarpeted passage, and on to the other end of the house.

"Her maid ain't worth much," muttered Mrs. Pine, as we paused outside the closed door of the new lodger's room.

The attendant admitted us. My first glance at her face gave me no favourable impression, and I felt instinctively that her mistress would receive little tenderness at her hands. It cost me an effort to enter the chamber; my heart throbbed fast as I crossed the threshold, uncertain what my reception would be. Ida sat by the bedside, on one of the hard rush-bottomed chairs. Her elbow rested on the bolster, and one hand was pressed upon her forehead. She must have heard the door open, but she never changed her position.

"I was told that you were not well," I said gently, "and I came to see if I could be of any use."

"Bessie, Bessie Mere?" she cried in a piercing tone. "Oh, take care of me Bessie as you used to do. I don't deserve it I know, but you will pity me. I am so ill." Her voice died away in a long wail.

"I will stay with you, Ida," I said soothingly. "But I think you must lie down on your bed and compose yourself."

She let me do with her as I would, only moaning and shivering at intervals. I laid her gently upon the pillow, and signed to the maid to withdraw.

"Have you sent my servant away?" she whispered, eagerly.

"Yes," I answered. "And now you will try to sleep, while I sit here and watch you?"

"Not yet, Bessie. Let me tell you all; I shall soon be too ill to talk."

"You must not excite yourself, Ida."

"Let me go on?" she pleaded. "Oh, Bessie, I have run away from Mrs. Burleigh's house, and I came to Axwood to meet George Lincoln. We were to have been privately married."

"Ida! surely not without your father's knowledge?"

"He has already refused his consent," she answered. "Mrs. Burleigh found out what was going on, and she objected to George very strongly. She said that the Lincolns were not what they seemed to be; she even called George a fortune-hunter. And then she wrote to papa, who is in Madeira, and he sent me a very harsh letter."

"But, Ida, you will not marry Mr. Lincoln? You will give up this mad scheme?"

"He has never come to me as he promised," she sobbed. "I have had no letter from him, although I have been staying at that miserable inn three days. And then I grew ill."

"Don't cry so bitterly," I said gently. "You have made a false step, but it is not irretrievable. When you are better you will return to Mrs. Burleigh, and give up all idea of this foolish marriage."

"I think I shall," she answered. "Write to her,

Bessie, and tell her I am here. And don't leave me; I do not like Norris, my maid."

I despatched a letter to Mrs. Burleigh at once informing her of Ida's illness, and begging her to send a competent nurse. She grew worse as the day wore on, and towards evening we sent for the village doctor. He came, and pronounced her disorder to be scarlet fever.

All night I watched by her side, while she tossed and moaned, and could not rest. Toward daybreak she fell into a quiet slumber, and I stole into Norris's room, intending to take a brief repose while the maid filled my place.

But no Norris was there; her bed had not been slept in. It was afterwards ascertained that she left the house during the night taking her mistress's jewel-case with her.

CHAPTER XIV.

A Confession and an Illness.

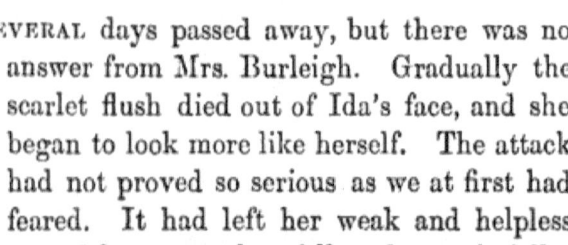

Several days passed away, but there was no answer from Mrs. Burleigh. Gradually the scarlet flush died out of Ida's face, and she began to look more like herself. The attack had not proved so serious as we at first had feared. It had left her weak and helpless as an infant; and her eyes often followed me wistfully, while I waited upon her and tended her.

"Bessie," said she one evening, when I sat down to rest in a chair near the window. "Do you believe it is really possible to forgive a very bitter injury?"

"Yes, Ida; it's very hard to do so, but by God's grace it is quite possible."

She was silent for a while. I listened to the whirring of insect wings through the still evening air, and watched a pearly cloud trailing across the dusky blue of the sky. Presently Ida spoke again in a tremulous voice.

"Bessie, I have not deserved all your kindness; I did you a cruel wrong. It was I who set Mrs. Daverill against you."

"I am not surprised," I answered, my eyes still fixed upon the bright pearly cloud. "I suspected that it was so."

"And you could return good for evil," she murmured. "Oh, how wicked I have been. How I hate myself. I will make a full confession, not only to you but to Mrs. Daverill."

I did not look at her, but I knew that she was weeping.

"I won't go back to our school days now," she went on. "I was mean and ungrateful to you then, but I did you no real harm. You were well rid of so troublesome a companion as I was."

How little she had fathomed the depths of my early love for her. I felt as I listened, that a nature like Ida's could never comprehend mine. She knew nothing of those strong affections which her unkindness had so sorely wounded. But I held my peace.

"I did not mean to injure you when first we met again," she continued; "but I became jealous, passionately jealous. You had grown so pretty, and your voice was so admired, that I felt myself put in the background. And it was Blanch Lincoln who first suggested to me a plan for damaging you in Mrs. Daverill's estimation. I should not have acceded to it —indeed I should not—if I hadn't seen that George was taken with you, and I feared——"

"Ida!" I interrupted, indignantly. "I never liked Mr. Lincoln; I have scarcely exchanged a dozen sentences with him. You must have been mad."

"I think I was," she answered sadly. "And now,

Bessie, even if you never speak to me again, I will tell you the whole story, and make all the reparation in my power. There is my blotting-book lying on the table. Will you bring it to me?"

I did so, and she took from it a letter, which she placed in my hands.

My own handwriting, and yet not mine! I noticed little turns and dots which my fingers had never made; but the words themselves, what were they?

In bold, dashing phrases, such as I had never used in my life, the writer appointed a clandestine interview with George Lincoln; and the note was signed with my full name, the envelope being addressed to 'George Lincoln, Esquire.'

I felt the hot blood rush into my face, as I clenched the letter in my grasp, and my breathing grew short and laboured. How dared they commit this forgery, an offence punishable by law? How could God have permitted such incredible wickedness to attain its end?

Why had He permitted it? For my own good. He saw that my feet had turned out of the narrow way, and, in love, He suffered the thorns to spring up in the by-path I had chosen. I remembered how He had led me, humbled in spirit, to my father's bedside, and there had shown me how poor and valueless were the things of 'this transitory life,' when seen in the sunlight of Heaven.

"Oh, Bessie, speak to me," sobbed Ida. "It was Blanch who wrote the note. She imitated your handwriting from the verses you copied for me. George, to do him justice, knew nothing of the plot. Blanch pretended to have found the letter on his dressing-table, and we persuaded Mrs. Daverill not to give her reasons for dismissing you. She could not do so, we told her, without involving Blanch in a quarrel with her brother."

What a deep scheme it was; clever in its iniquity.

"I do forgive you, Ida," I said, quietly coming to the bedside. "I pardon you from my heart. When you are strong and well, you will write your confession, as you promised, to Mrs. Daverill?"

"Oh, yes, yes, Bessie," she answered, kissing my hand.

Two more days went by, and then a fly stopped at the farm, and Mrs. Burleigh, with two attendants, hastily alighted. Her surprise at seeing me in the sick room was great, and she looked round in search of the missing Norris.

"As soon as I discovered Ida's flight," she explained, "I started off to bring her back; and, unfortunately, followed a wrong clue. I was away from home therefore, when your letter reached my house. But I did not expect to find that you had been Ida's nurse, Miss Mere."

"She has told me her story, Mrs. Burleigh," said I. "And I can assure you she has been safe from Mr. Lincoln; he has never appeared."

"He was utterly unable to fulfil his engagement," rejoined Mrs. Burleigh, laughing. "He has been arrested for debt."

The doctor was of opinion that Ida, weak as she

was, might be removed with safety in a short time. But not more than two days elapsed before Mrs. Burleigh and the London nurse decided to take her away. And she herself was most anxious to quit Axwood.

* * * * *

They were gone. Mrs. Pine had set the rooms in order, and I had returned to my own chamber. The Midsummer vacation had nearly expired, but I dared not go back to the school in Clapham, lest I should carry infection to the pupils. From time to time I had scrawled hurried notes to Aunt Esther, telling her of the new duty which had fallen to my lot. And now I sat down and wrote a lengthy statement of the case to Miss Goodwin herself. It was a laborious undertaking, that letter. Before it was finished I was conscious of languor and pain, and strange shiverings crept over me, although the summer sun was at its height. I resolutely completed my task, stamped and addressed the envelope, and then stretched myself upon my bed. By-and-by Mrs. Pine's entrance aroused me from an uneasy slumber.

"Dinner's been waiting some time, Miss," said she. "Bless me! Ain't you well?"

"Not quite, Mrs. Pine. My throat pains me much. I doubt if I can swallow any food."

"You're going to have the fever and no mistake!" rejoined my landlady, decidedly.

I knew that she was right. I raised myself from the pillow, pushed the hair away from my throbbing temples, and tried to think. I must let Aunt Esther know, that was the first thing to be done.

With shaky fingers I traced a few words to her, and lay down again. Then with a little moan I turned my face to the wall, knowing that a deadlier sickness than Ida's had laid its hold upon me and would not let me go.

*   *   *   *   *

A horror of great darkness, succeeding hours of painful half-consciousness, and then a strange revisiting of old scenes and old places. I seemed sometimes to be whirled through the air with fearful rapidity, while the cathedral spire and the house-roofs of Priorsbury lay far below. And sometimes the delirium took another turn. I stood on the banks of the river without a bridge, hearing my father calling to me across the dark water, telling me to be of good courage, for companies of 'shining ones' were waiting on the other side, to lead me to the Celestial City.

But there came at last an hour when my senses returned; slowly and painfully the mists and vague dreams cleared away, and then I became conscious of a voice in the chamber uttering earnest words of prayer.

"Aunt Esther," I said, in a faint whisper, when the voice had ceased. She came and bent tenderly over me; but the tones were not hers.

Then, by degrees, I began to regain a little strength. I was pillowed up in bed, and could venture to ask a few questions.

"Aunty, who was praying for me? Will he come again?"

"Yes, my child, he *will* come again. He is a good man, and has comforted me as no one else could have done."

"But what is his name, Aunty? Who is he?"

"His name is Lyvian, and he is a clergyman. Now, dearie, you musn't talk any more."

CHAPTER XV.

Conclusion.

IT seemed from the first as if Mr. Lyvian knew all about me; understanding my sorrows and difficulties as no one had ever done before, saving perhaps my father. He was not the regular clergyman of Axwood, but had come to stay in the place and take charge of the parish while the Vicar was away. It was a change and a rest to him, he said, for his own church was in the east end of London.

Days of utter peace and quietness followed my illness. My new friend came daily to visit me, reading to me when I could not read for myself; or talking as Evangelist talked to the pilgrims on their journey.

"I had almost thought," I said to him one day, "that I had come to the end of my pilgrimage. I have been down to the very brink of the river which has no bridge, and I felt half sorry not to cross over to that other side where my father waits for me."

"That is hardly right," he answered gravely.

"You are very young yet, and God has plenty of work for you to do in the world."

"But I am so lonely," I said sadly. "My aunt and I can only meet sometimes. I have to live amongst strangers. It did not seem hard to do this while my father was living, I could go to him when I needed his counsel. It has been another world since he died."

"You have an unfailing Friend and Guide," replied Mr. Lyvian. "One who will watch every step of your pilgrimage, and lead you to His house at last. And in the mean time He will use you, if you are willing to do something for Him. Can you not try to bring other pilgrims into the right way? Surely your journey to the Celestial City need not be a lonely one."

"I am afraid I have never thought of doing that," I said musingly. "I have been much occupied of late with my own sorrows."

"The happiest person in the world is one who has—

> 'A heart at leisure from itself,
> To soothe and sympathise,'"

returned my new friend. "Try to study the characters of those around you and find out the way to win them. You will have many opportunities of doing this in a large school. You do not know how great an influence you possess over your pupils' minds; do not let so much power lie passive when it should be active."

These restful days soon came to an end, and I

went back to Clapham. Miss Goodwin had found a temporary substitute, still keeping my former post open for me. It was a little hard at first, to take up my duties again, for my strength was scarcely equal to them; but by degrees the tasks grew easier; and then I set about that other kind of work of which Mr. Lyvian had spoken. How I succeeded in it, need not be told here, for my story must hasten on to its close.

One day I received a letter from Mrs. Cravenhurst, enclosing one written to her by Mrs. Daverill. Ida had fulfilled her promise, and had made an open confession of the cruel way in which she had injured me. Mrs. Daverill was full of remorse, and she begged the Dean's wife to persuade me to return to my first situation. But this I declined to do, although my former pupil and her mother came personally to entreat me. I suited Miss Goodwin; my present abode was near Aunt Esther, and I felt a positive reluctance to go back to the old scenes. They made me promise, however, to visit them when I could spare time; and this promise I gladly kept.

It was from the Daverills that I heard of the great disgrace which had fallen on the Lincolns. Mr. Lincoln the elder was at the head of a well-known banking firm, and was looked upon as a rich and honourable man. But it transpired that he and his son had been for some years defrauding the public, a crash came, and ruin ensued. And Blanch, the haughty, spoiled girl, was reduced to actual poverty.

* * * * *

Another Midsummer vacation, and I went to Priorsbury to spend it at the Deanery. I found the beautiful old house and its inmates unchanged, and rambled about in my old haunts with a kind of sorrowful joy, still thinking of the dear one I had lost. But Mrs. Cravenhurst would not let me have leisure to grieve too much.

"Bessie," said she, one bright afternoon, when we were wandering together under the Cathedral elms, "is there not one friend whom you would like to meet again?"

"Yes," I answered, without hesitation, "Mr. Lyvian. You know I have told you all about him, and how good he was to me."

"Then you will see him this evening at dinner. The Dean has made his acquaintance, and likes him very much."

I did see him. He spent a week with the Cravenhursts, and a happy week it was to me. I was never weary of hearing all that he had to tell of his work in London, how the true Light was shining in dark places; and the Dean listened thoughtfully, thinking perhaps that the lot of a wealthy cathedral dignitary, and the life of an overworked London incumbent, had not many points of similarity.

Again I went back to my school duties, finding them a little dull and tame. But I remembered Who had given them to me, and I did my best to fulfil them all.

*　　　*　　　*　　　*　　　*

Yet another Midsummer, and I was invited to the

Deanery once more. My heart was lighter now, and I think that my face had grown brighter; the sorrows of the past had subdued me, but they had not made me a melancholy woman. I had the same delight in all beautiful things that characterized me as a child; I still felt the old keen pleasure in trifles which many wiser folk pass by unnoticed. And I even enjoyed that railway journey to Priorsbury; although it was a sultry day, and I was seated in a second-class carriage, as befitted a humble governess who could not afford to travel 'first.'

The day was closing in as we drew near Priorsbury, and I can remember how eagerly I glanced from the window to catch a glimpse of the tall spire. I saw it, piercing the evening clouds, lifting its fair height above the sweet green gloom of rich woods; and the happy tears filled my eyes. And then, as the train swept round a curve in the line, the ancient city itself was fully revealed to my gaze. It lay enfolded in the golden mist of a midsummer sunset; the soft thymy hills encompassing it on every side, and the familiar buildings all glorified in that tender light. I thought of another City whose "builder and maker is God;" I thought of the saints who tread its shining streets and join in its everlasting song. And I remembered that my father was among the number of those who had come out of "great tribulation, and had washed their robes, and made them white in the blood of the Lamb."

Captain Ashburn was there too; the brave soldier, and true-hearted Christian gentleman, who had wrestled not only 'against flesh and blood,' but had fought the good fight and kept the faith. Ay, and poor Jack, the humble penitent, and thousands of others who had fallen in that bitter Crimean strife; mighty and lowly, victor and vanquished, follower and chief. For that City is vaster than our feeble fancy dreams of, and He who reigns therein hath willed that 'His house shall be full.' The great multitude whom no man can number, are pressing upwards by divers paths to meet at last in the same eternal Home.

So I thought of them all with a full heart; those who were still on their way thither, and those who had already reached the goal, and I prayed that I too might enter into that rest.

> "They climbed the steep ascent of heaven,
> Through peril, toil, and pain;
> O God, to us may grace be given
> To follow in their train."

I reached my destination, and was welcomed with all the old kindliness. The calm days went and came, and I found myself wondering if Mr. Lyvian would come to the Deanery again? But for some inexplicable reason I could not ask the question. Once or twice his name was mentioned, and then I fancied that I saw Mrs. Cravenhurst exchange a meaning glance with her husband. I was puzzled, therefore, and kept silence.

One evening I had strayed out of the house alone, and sought my ancient haunt under the walls of the Cathedral. The place was still and sweet. The green elm-boughs swayed languidly to and fro, and the shifting light and shade made a tremulous pattern on the soft grass. I went straight to the gray tomb which had so often been my seat in childish days, and then and there I fell into a musing fit that lasted some time.

The rooks cawed loudly, high above my head, circling about the time-worn towers and venerable trees, but I heeded them not. The shadows grew longer and longer, and as the sun sank lower, a golden bar of light slanted across the clasped hands that lay idly upon my lap, but I did not stir. So absorbed was I in meditation that my ears were deaf to the sound of footsteps coming towards me, and I started to hear Mr. Lyvian's voice at my side.

"Well," he asked cheerfully, when the first greetings had passed between us, "has your path been lonely of late, or have you been joined by many other pilgrims?"

"Not by many," I answered, a little sadly. "The way is too rugged to be pleasant, and I am often reminded of the words of Thomas à Kempis, 'Jesus has many lovers of His heavenly kingdom, but few are willing to bear His cross.'"

"That is an old experience," he said. And then, still holding my hand in his, he added gently, "But you need not be desolate, Bessie."

"No," I replied, "I cannot be desolate while I have a Friend in heaven; yet one sometimes longs for earthly companionship."

"Then let us walk together in the narrow way

side by side, as husband and wife?" He waited for a reply, but words did not come readily to my lips. I looked up for an instant into his face, and he knew what that answer was that I could not speak.

* * * * *

I have been married three years to-day. The first part of my wedded life was spent in the London parsonage; there in the very heart of the great city, my little son was born, and there I gladly shared my husband's labours. But now Mr. Lyvian is a canon of Priorsbury Cathedral, and three months of each year will be passed in the dear old place.

Our house is in the stone-paved alley. It is early in May, and the lilacs and laburnums and chestnuts are all in bloom in the Bishop's garden, and the blossoms trail over the high wall in front of my window. I can hear the rooks holding a clamorous confabulation, talking in the hoarse, familiar tones; and Aunt Esther drops her work to listen to them.

I have had a letter to-day from Rosa Daverill, containing tidings of the Sedgeworths. They have gone to live in Italy, for both Ida and her father are in delicate health. My poor schoolfellow; wealth did not bring her all the bliss that she expected! Rosa is coming to pay us a visit next week; her affection for me has never changed, and we are preparing to give her a warm welcome to the Close.

What a bright fresh day it is! My boy is at play with his nurse among the green mounds, under the shadowy elms. There too, I doubt not I shall find Clara Cravenhurst taking her morning stroll. I will

"My boy is at play with his nurse among the green mounds."

go and seek her, link my arm in hers, and pace slowly up and down, as we used to do long ago. For her and for me the old place teems with memories; but the present is full of peaceful happiness, and we do not talk about that far-off past.

It is early yet, and as I pass into the cloisters, I hear the clear voices of the choristers; they are practising an anthem, and the sweet notes come drifting towards me. I pause for a moment, and then steal through a side door into the nave of the Cathedral. The great church is very quiet, and the soft coloured lights from the deeply-stained windows fall here and there. Above me rises the mighty vaulted roof where the gray shadows always linger; around me are the tall columns and the sculptured angel-faces that smiled on the little Bessie Mere of years gone by. And from some remote part of the building, those silver tones float down the stately aisles:

"Some put their trust in chariots and some in horses, but we will remember the name of the Lord our God."

My heart echoes that solemn strain. I will remember Him, and all the way that He hath led me, for "like as a father pitieth his own children, even so is the Lord merciful unto them that fear Him."

In all time of my tribulation His grace was sufficient for me; His strength was made perfect in my weakness: and now in the season of my earthly prosperity,

I will turn unto Him, and pray that He will ever keep my feet in the narrow path that leadeth to everlasting life.

So with this prayer in my soul, and with His holy name still lingering on my lips, I leave the old sanctuary, and come forth again into the fragrant air and golden morning sunshine.

Here first began the story of my life;—here let it end,

"UNDER THE GRAY WALLS."

REWARD & GIFT BOOKS

PUBLISHED BY THE

SUNDAY SCHOOL UNION,

56, OLD BAILEY, LONDON,

AND

SOLD BY ALL BOOKSELLERS.

RECENTLY ISSUED,

Illustrated by Numerous Engravings,

FROM TENT TO PALACE;

OR,

THE STORY OF JOSEPH.

BY BENJAMIN CLARKE,

Author of "First Heroes of the Cross," "Life of Jesus for Young People," etc.

Price 3s. 6d. cloth boards.

Catalogue of Reward and Gift Books.

Copiously Illustrated, with Coloured Map. (*Third Thousand.*) *Price* 4s.

THE FIRST HEROES OF THE CROSS.
BY BENJAMIN CLARKE,
Author of "From Tent to Palace," "The Life of Jesus, for Young People," &c.

THE DEATH OF EUTYCHUS.

The windows of upper rooms overhung the streets; and in the recess a raised seat, or divan, was usually placed, and when occasion required, a seat above the divan, level with the window. On this raised seat, during the evening, sat a young man named Eutychus, close to the open window, glad to get all the air he could; but in spite of his favourable position, overcome by the heat of the room, and perhaps wearied out with the day's toil, he fell asleep. Paul had been long preaching, and it was now past midnight. He knew this was the last time he should see the disciples here, and they knew it too; all were therefore reluctant for Paul to discontinue his address. He was not only preaching the Gospel, but relating his adventures in connection therewith; and those, therefore, who knew the apostle best were most anxious to hear from him all they could.

Catalogue of Reward and Gift Books.

THE ORPHAN AND THE FOUNDLING;
OR, ALONE IN THE WORLD.

By EMMA LESLIE, Author of "Harry Lawley," &c.

Crown 8vo.   Engravings.   (Sixth Thousand.)   2s., cloth boards.

ONE BY HERSELF.
BY MRS. CLARA LUCAS BALFOUR.

(In the Press.)

Catalogue of Reward and Gift Books.

THE SECRET DRAWER.

By the Author of "Alice Middleton: a Story of the Days of Mary and Elizabeth."

Crown 8vo. Illustrated. (Sixth Thousand.) 2s., cloth, handsomely bound.

"A touching tale of the Garibaldini and of Italian life in London. . . . It is handsomely got up."—*Freeman.*

"Unlike many tales of mystery, its tone and tendency are excellent."—*Literary World.*

MEN WORTH IMITATING;

Or, Brief Sketches of Noble Lives.

By W. H. GROSER, B.Sc., F.G.S.,

Author of "Facts and Fancies," "The Teacher's Model," &c., &c.

Crown 8vo. Illustrated. (Fourth Thousand.) Price 2s., cloth boards.

"The author endeavours to elevate the minds of the young by setting before them deeds of moral grandeur and excellence, so that by learning to admire they may be incited to imitate."—*Literary World.*

"Exceedingly well fitted for young boys."—*Nonconformist.*

"In every way to be commended."—*Sword and Trowel.*

FAITH HARROWBY;

Or, The Smuggler's Cave.

By SARAH DOUDNEY, Author of "The Beautiful Island."

Crown 8vo. Illustrated. (Fourth Thousand.) Price 2s., handsomely bound.

UNDER GRAY WALLS.

By SARAH DOUDNEY,

Author of "Faith Harrowby," &c.

Crown 8vo. Illustrated. 2s. cloth boards.

PERCY RAYDON;

Or, Self-Conquest.

By EMMA LESLIE,

Author of "Harry Lawley," "The Orphan and the Foundling," &c.

Crown 8vo. Beautifully Illustrated. 2s., cloth boards.

Catalogue of Reward and Gift Books.

HARRY LAWLEY AND HIS MAIDEN AUNTS.

By EMMA LESLIE, Author of "The Orphan and the Foundling," &c.

Crown 8vo. Illustrated. (Sixth Thousand.) 2s. cloth.

"It is a well-told story, with a real sympathy for, and understanding of, a boy's feelings and temptations."—*Literary Churchman.*

LILLIE'S PIGEON.

"He called at the gardener's cottage as he passed, and found Lillie feeding her pet pigeon."

Catalogue of Reward and Gift Books.

THE TRUE HERO:
A STORY OF THE DAYS OF WILLIAM PENN.
By W. H. G. KINGSTON.

Crown 8vo.   Illustrated.   Price 2s. 6d., handsomely bound.

Nearly ready,

CONSTANCIA'S HOUSEHOLD:
A Story of the Spanish Reformation.
By EMMA LESLIE,
Author of "Percy Raydon," "The Orphan and the Foundling," &c., &c.

Catalogue of Reward and Gift Books.

OLD OAK FARM. By the late Rev. T. T. HAVERFIELD, B.D. Fcap. 8vo. Engravings. (Sixth Thousand.) 1s. 6d., cloth boards.

"The subject is very attractive, developing the incidents and *exposé* of a Jesuit plot. The work is nicely got up and illustrated, and ought to be widely read."—*Bucks Chronicle.*

BREAKING THE RULES: a Tale of School-boy Life. By Mrs. H. B. PAULL, Author of "Miss Herbert's Keys," &c. Fcap. 8vo. With Engravings. (Fourth Thousand.) 1s. 6d., cloth boards.

"The only regret one feels in laying this story down is that there is not more of it."—*Hastings and St. Leonards Gazette.*

MISS HERBERT'S KEYS. By Mrs. H. B. PAULL, Author of "Breaking the Rules," &c. Fcap. 8vo. Engravings. (Fifth Thousand.) 1s. 6d., cloth boards.

Catalogue of Reward and Gift Books.

ALICE MIDDLETON: a Story of the Days of Mary and Elizabeth. By the Author of "The Secret Drawer." (Fourth Thousand.) Price 10d.

ANCIENT NINEVEH: a Story for the Young. A new and improved Edition. Price 1s.

BEAUTIFUL ISLAND (THE) and Other Stories. With Engravings. (Fifth Thousand.) Price 1s., cloth boards.

EXILES (THE) and Other Tales. With Engravings. (Fifth Thousand.) Price 1s. 6d., cloth boards.

FACTS AND FANCIES: a Book of Sketches and Counsels for Young People. 1s. 6d., cloth boards.

RICHARD OWEN'S CHOICE; or, Master and Servant. By Mrs. JOSEPH LAMB. (Fourth Thousand.) Limp cloth, 6d.; gilt edges, 8d.

TOMMY'S MARBLES, and other Stories. With Engravings. (Seventh Thousand.) Price 1s. 4d., cloth boards.

CATALOGUES OF THE PUBLICATIONS OF THE SUNDAY SCHOOL UNION MAY BE OBTAINED ON APPLICATION.

www.ingramcontent.com/pod-product-compliance
Lightning Source LLC
Chambersburg PA
CBHW021939160426
43195CB00011B/1152